D1635608

Leadership with Consciousness

TONY HUMPHREYS

Attic

First published in 2011 by Attic Press
Attic Press is an imprint of Cork University Press
Youngline Industrial Estate
Pouladuff Road, Togher
Cork, Ireland

© Tony Humphreys

All rights reserved. No part of this book may be reprinted
or reproduced or utilised in any electronic, mechanical or other
means, now known or hereafter invented, including photocopying and
recording or otherwise, without either the prior written permission
of the publisher or a licence permitting restricted copying in
Ireland issued by the Irish Copyright Licensing Agency Ltd,
25 Denzille Lane, Dublin 2.

The right of Tony Humphreys to be identified as author of this Work
has been asserted by him in accordance with Copyright and Related
Rights Acts 2000 to 2007.

British Library Cataloguing in Publication Data
A CIP catalogue record for this book is available from the British Library.

ISBN-13: 978-185594-219-9
Printed in the UK by MPG Books
Typeset by Tower Books, Ballincollig, Co. Cork

www.corkuniversitypress.com

Contents

Please hear what I'm not saying

Don't be fooled by me.

Don't be fooled by the face that I wear. For I wear a mask.

I wear a thousand masks that I am afraid to take off, and none of them is the real me.

So don't be fooled by me, I'm good at pretending.

I give the impression that I'm cool and confident, but inside, it's different.

I'm not in command.

I'm often confused, lonely and desperately need someone to understand me.

But I hide and I don't want anyone to know.

That's why I frantically create a mask to hide behind,

I'm afraid to show the real me.

I'm afraid that you will not accept me.

I'm afraid that you will think less of me and laugh at me.

You see, deep down, I'm afraid that I'm nothing, that I'm no good,

And if you knew me, you would reject me.

So I play my game, my pretending game, and thus begins my parade of masks.

My life becomes a front to protect the real me.

I chatter idly to you about everything but tell you nothing of what's going on inside me – my fears, my worries, my doubts.

So when I'm talking, please listen carefully and try to hear what I'm not saying, what I'd like to say but I can't.

I'd like to be genuine, honest and sincere, but I cannot without your help.

My trust grows very slowly, so you will have to be patient with me.

Each time you are kind, gentle and encouraging, each time you try to understand, I am given new hope and I start believing in myself in a new way.

You let me see it's o.k. to be me.

So I can take off the mask and be happy in your company, I can let
   you see the real me.
Who am I, you may wonder? I am someone you know very well.
For I am every man and woman you meet.

Charles C. Finn
(*abbreviated version*)
September 1966

Introduction

When giving a presentation at an international conference on human resources management I was asked several times 'what's a clinical psychologist doing at a HR conference? My reply was to say that in preparing for the conference and in studying the prevailing ideas that determine the attitudes and practices of HR personnel, I found absolutely no reference to the fact that we have an *unconscious* and that the very troubled and troubling behaviours that people show are created in that sphere of the mind. A further reality is that unless what is in the unconscious comes into *consciousness* no change in an individual's behaviour can occur – be he or she a CEO, a manager, an employee, an entrepreneur. Another reason I put forward for the dire necessity for a clinical psychologist to speak with HR personnel is that there appears very little recognition that it is not a system – a work organisation – a bank, a multinational organisation, a financial institution – that perpetrates unethical, unfair, arrogant, superior and aggressive strategies – it is *individuals.* It has been a very cleverly designed *unconscious* strategy to blame the system – be it government, health services, church, work organisations, schools and colleges – for society's ills. But if truth be told – if truth comes to consciousness – it was individual politicians, bankers, leaders, pope, cardinals, bishops, priests that have brought our country to its knees spiritually, socially and economically. It was very apparent that the economic recession was not due to economic factors alone but arose from powerful emotional processes that have not been even remotely addressed.

What has also been so apparent since the recession started is the absence of accountability and authenticity by the key individuals who are responsible for the troubled state we are in. These absences are not surprising; the most powerful unconscious defence mechanism that individuals form is *denial*. When a person is in a state of denial, no matter how devastating their actions are in the eyes of others, he or she does not even remotely see the havoc they are creating. This is very difficult for those people who are at the receiving end of the neglect, and unless they come to understand the power and genius of the unconscious mind, they will continue to judge, blame, condemn and witch-hunt those who have and are perpetrating such devastation. The irony of it is that those of us who blame and judge others and are waiting for them to change are also operating from an unconscious defensive place – known technically as *projection* – and that we are just as stuck as those who are in denial. No change is possible unless a shift in consciousness occurs either in those who are in denial or those who are projecting.

The reality is that those individuals who are in *denial* are in terror of being judged, blamed and abandoned by everyone. Such terror of abandonment would have arisen in the childhood years where unconditional holding was not present and the terror of not being loved would have driven them to do anything to please their parents and teachers – 'be perfect', 'be clever', 'be a good boy', 'be the best', 'don't let us down', 'prove yourself to me', 'live your life for me'. Any possible fall from these impossible conditions would evoke inward turmoil and the necessity to unconsciously escalate defences that would eliminate or reduce the possibility of falling off their pedestals. Examples of these defences would be perfectionism, obsessions and compulsions, superiority, addictions to study, to getting things right, extreme upset when something goes wrong (it is very difficult to be aggressive with a child who is overwhelmingly upset – what a clever defence!) or major temper tantrums and destructive responses when things go wrong (again a powerful defence that distracts the parents and teachers from the 'failure' and puts their attention on managing the aggressive outbursts). The question to ask here is: how many of these defensive responses do you recognise in yourself and in many of our leaders and managers? The most common type of management is of a bullying, arrogant, superior and critical nature and the most common experience of employees is of anonymity. Indeed, most employees, when possible, leave their jobs, not because of the job itself, but because of the manager's aggressive and depersonalising behaviours.

When leaders and managers are stuck in a defensive cycle – and it appears the majority are – no consciousness of their unconscious defences will emerge, unless they encounter non-judgement, understanding, unconditional regard and encouragement to be authentic and real. How wise – any hint of judgement and rejection only serves to escalate their childhood fears of abandonment.

The challenge is: who is going to provide such a safe holding? Certainly, those of us who blame and judge them – who are unconsciously projecting – are in no mature place to help. The reality is that we are in need of as much help as those who are in denial. It follows from this that it is necessary for most of us to encounter a non-judgemental and unconditional relationship before a shift to consciousness and maturity will emerge. There have been wonderful unconsciously formed illusions that most people are party to – that education, age, wealth, status are indices of maturity. Not so, what is characteristic of maturity is a solid sense of self, a belief and confidence in self, independence, and a responsibility for self and all of one's actions, towards oneself and others. Such a maturity is a rare phenomenon but is direly needed if we are to progress from the very troubled Ireland we are currently experiencing. The fostering of personal maturity is a key aim of this book – the unrestricted personal growth of each individual person – and how this can be achieved in the key holding worlds we live in – family, community, school, workplace and third-level educational institutions.

It is not just leaders and managers who need to be targeted for personal maturity, but each and every one of us. There is none of us who do not need to examine our lives – how we feel, think, what we say and do – and those of us who claim that 'I'm alright Jack' need the most help! It is a fact that personal effectiveness and personal maturity determine professional effectiveness. While this book's primary focus is on leaders and managers – because it is how they are in themselves and the amount of emotional baggage they carry that largely determines the ethos of an organisation – the book is a must for each and every one of us.

The genius of our unconscious – how it powerfully and creatively protects us from emotional pain – when released into consciousness becomes an immense driving force for good in the world. Those leaders and managers, who achieve a shift in unconscious genius moving to consciousness will have advantages far and away beyond the colleagues who are still imprisoned by their fears and insecurities and hidden behind the walls of their defences. The tragedy is that while there is a comfort in being hidden – it protects – it is an absolute calamity not to be found, not to come into consciousness of your profound and powerful unique and individual human nature. Indeed, it is a great threat to all of us when people present themselves wearing a thousand masks and not revealing their true nature.

I'm sure it is becoming clear that leadership and management with the genius of consciousness present is a radically different phenomenon to leadership and management with the genius of unconsciousness present. The latter is highly threatening, the former majorly empowering, respectful, equal, loving, understanding, compassionate and patient. Management with consciousness does not excuse irresponsibility, but what it does is provide the safe opportunities for responsibility to emerge. In the waiting period it ensures that nobody is at risk from the defensive behaviours of the person who requires a shift to consciousness.

What is also addressed in the book is training for managers and leaders – indeed training for all employees. Training needs to provide the safe opportunities by trainers who largely operate from a place of consciousness. In this regard, a list of the qualities of conscious management is provided. It is a matter of these qualities emerging, as the manager experiences a shift from a defensive unconsciousness to an open place of consciousness. These qualities cannot be rote learned; they are parts of our nature that have lain hidden in response to the threats of giving expression to them. Ultimately, conscious self-management becomes the basis of effective conscious management of others. Furthermore, the shift to consciousness, especially in males, leads to a management that involves both head and heart. Men's fear of emotional expression and difficulty with emotional receptivity has significantly limited their effectiveness as leaders and managers. It is accurate to say that *affectiveness* leads to greater effectiveness, as a person is operating out from the fullness of their nature. Women have tended to operate more from heart than from head and this reduces their effectiveness. Effective management is not a gender issue – it is a human issue and a matter of maturity, and the challenge to come into maturity applies to both men and women. The fact that the top leadership and management positions have largely been occupied by men has created a reaction to males as leaders, but there is no guarantee that women will do any better, unless they are at a higher level of consciousness.

Training to effect personal maturity needs to be of a *face-to-face* nature, and post-training follow-ups are essential. Training needs to be directed at the whole person so that trainees will come to consciously see:

- that the unconscious exists
- how to raise consciousness in self and others
- how to recognise and understand the creativity of unconscious defensive responses in self and others
- how to create a work ethos where employees are engaged, rather than disengaged or 'constantly against everything' (CAVE dwellers)
- how to communicate from the inside (an 'I' place) out
- how to create an ethos of emotional and social safety so that employees can speak openly about their fears, ideas and values
- how to develop a person-centred approach in their management practice.

The suffocation of individuality and the aggressive depersonalisation of employees and, indeed, of customers, creates a dark work ethos. Employees largely complain of anonymity and a fear of bringing their individuality, own beliefs and values inside the organisation's door! Managers can only create a 'people before profits' approach when they operate out from a sense of their individuality. The responsibility for managers and leaders to inhabit their individuality is an urgent one.

This book reflects a synthesis of theory and practice and rests on the solid theoretical foundation of the psychology of the self. This theoretical approach has been validated and deepened through my long professional practice with individuals and groups in a wide range of settings, including the family, the school, the community, the workplace and third-level educational institutions. Some of the insights presented originated in earlier writings of mine.

The book is a collection of published articles and some unpublished material, grouped under seven chapter headings, and the width and breadth of the topics are as follows:

- the nature of unconsciousness and consciousness
- the defence mechanisms that seriously interrupt political, social and economic progress
- the concept of individual responsibility as opposed to blaming the system
- the concern that males dominate leadership and managerial positions!
- what lies hidden behind defence mechanisms and the process of bringing these to consciousness
- the amazing power of the human psyche
- the need for leadership and management that is both affective and effective
- the fact that both managers and leaders are constantly spilling the beans on their hidden vulnerabilities for those who have the mature ears to hear and eyes to see!
- the differences between leaders and managers
- the addictions to success, work, status, power and money
- gender issues in management
- training for mature leadership and management
- mature people-managing

- the effects of bullying and passivity on individuals and organisational progress
- the difference between boundaries and defences
- mature communication
- governorship of self
- the healing power of stress
- the creativity of conflict
- the nature and challenge of accountability.

Chapter Seven presents an outline of training for consciousness and concludes with an overview.

1 Genius of Unconsciousness

The Story Behind What We Do

Everybody has a story and each person's story is a unique autobiography and only that person fully knows their story.

However, some aspects of a person's story may be known only at an unconscious level and this hidden world will only become available to consciousness when the person finds adequate emotional and social safety, initially with another and, subsequently, within self.

The story of a person's life is not the events he or she encounters – for example, difficult birth, loving mother, emotionless home, conditional loving, violent father, possessive mother, kind grandparent, affirming teacher. The story consists of the person's inner responses to these events. What is amazing in a family or classroom or workplace is that each person responds in a unique way to situations that arise. This means that each child has a different mother and a different father, each student a different teacher, each employee a different manager and each voter a different politician. This makes total sense because when two individuals interact, inevitably, their interaction will be of a unique nature. Parents are powerful witnesses to how each child is completely different from the other and this happens whether children are reared in benign or difficult circumstances.

However, when children are reared in violating circumstances their individuality is expressed through the unique formation of very powerful defensive behaviours that are designed on the one hand to reduce the frequently encountered threats to their well-being, and on the other to bring to the attention of any mature

Leabharlanna Fhine Gall

adult in their lives their deeply troubled interiority. Children who experience a stable and loving family also express their individuality and develop a repertoire of open and creative responses that are different to those of the other siblings. Another way of putting it is that children whose wellbeing is jeopardised daily are ingenious in the ways that they repress (hide away) what aspects of their individual self that they dare not exhibit, while children whose wellbeing is unconditionally held are ingenious in the ways that they express and manifest their individuality, ensuring that they are not confused with anybody else within the family.

As an adult, each of us has a responsibility to occupy our own individuality. To do that, we need to become aware of our unconscious and conscious responses. You may well ask, are we not always conscious of what we feel, think, say and do? Certainly, you may notice that you can be aggressive, violent, shy, timid or manipulative but you may not be conscious of the sources of those defensive responses. Unless these sources are uncovered, your threatening responses towards yourself or towards others will continue. Consciousness requires that we own, understand and are accountable to our inner and outer behaviours and that, when the responses are defensive (as opposed to mature) in nature, that we make new mature choices and take new mature actions.

Take the example of a manager in the workplace that bullies and intimidates other employees. When confronted, he is likely to justify and rationalise his threatening responses by, for example, 'nobody would do anything around here without being shouted and ranted at' or 'being bullied did me no harm as a child'. However, when that manager compassionately understands the bullying behaviour as an unconscious creation arising from unresolved fears within himself – for instance, fear of failure, fear of what others think, fear of letting down his parents – it is likely that a consciousness will emerge of the real threat that he is posing to the wellbeing of employees. Once that consciousness is present, new choices and new actions are now possible towards himself and the employees. Uncovering the story of what led to the bullying is not an attempt to dilute the serious emotional threat that bullying poses – sadly, over sixty suicides occur annually in Ireland as a result of bullying in the workplace. On the contrary, it is my belief and my experience that unless the person who bullies becomes conscious of his hidden self-esteem issues, his defensive behaviour will continue and is likely to escalate when outside pressures increase. Change is only possible when what lies hidden is brought to the surface and what it was in his story that led to the creative development of bullying as a means of withstanding hurt. Individuals who bully need the support to stand with themselves, so that they are no longer dependent on others standing with them. The overt intention of bullying is to ensure control, but the covert intention is to draw attention to the urgent need to be in control of self and to support others to do likewise.

Whatever the threatening behaviours in which we engage, either towards self or others, the unravelling of their purpose can only be found in the examination of one's story and the discovery of what the defensive responses are doing for you that you need to be doing for yourself.

The Power of Vulnerability

I hesitate to use the word 'vulnerability' because it is generally associated with weakness and helplessness. Nevertheless, some individuals describe themselves as 'vulnerable' most probably knowing that others will perceive them as weak, dependent and not able to stand on their own two feet. However, there is a wonderful wisdom and strength to this unconscious strategy – making it far from being weak – in that it powerfully places the responsibility on others to 'look after' the person. As creative, ingenious and unique human beings I believe that we are never weak, but in the face of threats to our wellbeing we unconsciously form protective strategies to reduce or offset such threats. It is important to understand that these protectors are formed *unconsciously* and it is at some later stage when we encounter the emotional, social and intellectual safety to be real and authentic that we will allow such knowledge to rise to *consciousness*, make new choices and take alternative and progressive actions.

Is what I'm saying true? Can we actually believe that people's passivity, anxiety, helplessness, manipulation, emotional and physical withdrawal and hypersensitivity are powers beyond measure? Many people in the caring professions also refer to such individuals as being vulnerable and I believe miss the point that, within the threatening context these people have lived and are still encountering, they have found the best possible means of surviving the defensive behaviours of significant individuals in their lives – mother, father, sibling, teacher, grandparent, peer (as a child), or mother, father, sibling, employer, friend, lover, partner (as an adult). Whether it is a professional helper or another person who labels the person as 'vulnerable', they too do so unconsciously, and thereby their labelling has the effect of reinforcing the protectors of that person. What is happening here is that professional care workers or others are in a protected place themselves and when protectors meet protectors, inevitably they will escalate. However, were the observer to notice and affirm the creativity and power of the protective behaviour, the person seeking help, rather than encountering further threats, would experience emotional, social and intellectual safety. In experiencing such safe holdings, the person who is undoubtedly suffering may now allow what is unconscious to rise to consciousness so that authentic rather than further protective action can be taken. For example, a person who has asthma, in the embrace of unconditional love may allow consciousness to emerge of how she was rarely, if ever, allowed to breathe her own life and had always felt fearful and constricted by the perfectionism and lack of warmth displayed by her mother. The new choices to be made are to create inclusive ties with herself and, as that happens, to cut the restrictive ties with her mother, to be determined to live her own life and to love herself in the ways, sadly, that her mother was not in a place to offer.

What is interesting is that when it comes to describing a person who is vicious, aggressive, dominating, controlling, arrogant and authoritarian, we do not use the term 'vulnerable', even though the person is every bit as fearful. This is, true to what I believe, equally clever because aggressive-type responses are more obviously threatening to our presence and authentic actions than the more passive-type responses that fall under the motivated 'misnomer' of 'vulnerable'. The labels we put on those who are aggressive are counter-aggressive in nature, the hope being that these will stop the person in their violating tracks and, thereby, reduce the threats to our wellbeing. However, individuals who are aggressive and violent equally need our understanding and compassion because they too are hiding their wholeness and certain aspects of self-expression.

In examining any human behaviour, unless a person is in a heightened state of consciousness, what you see and hear is not what you need 'to get' – on the contrary, it is what you don't see that needs to be uncovered. Protective responses are designed to cover up what you dare not show. Uncovering what is hidden is only possible when unconditional love and belief in the person is present. This is as true in understanding ourselves as it is in the understanding of another. The word 'understand' when hyphenated – under-stand – indicates the necessity to get below the 'stand' (the protective behaviour) of self or another. Responding to the face value of what you or another says or does results in what needs to come to consciousness receding further into darkness. The reality is that such defensive responding is common in most homes, classrooms, workplaces, the Dail and churches. We are complex beings, powerful in guarding the unique diamond of Self and we will only allow spontaneous and authentic expression of our true and individual nature where there is the persistent presence of safe holdings.

The Roots of Inferiority

When Eleanor Roosevelt (Roosevelt, 1950) made her now famous quote 'Nobody makes me feel inferior without my permission', she missed an important aspect of human behaviour and that is that we have an *unconscious* mind that the Self employs creatively and powerfully in times of threat to our wellbeing.

The implication from Eleanor Roosevelt's quote is that the person who encounters a 'putdown' from another person *consciously* internalises it and, thereby, allows the other to define his worth. Carrying this understanding to its logical conclusion, it would equally be true to say that 'Nobody makes me feel good without my permission.'

It appears to me that a deeper observation is required which looks to answer the question: What is it that leads a person to react and seemingly internalise another person's comments – derogatory or complimentary – as being about him? The mature person knows that whatever another person says is 100 per cent *about* that person, *belongs* to and is *for* that person. For example, if somebody calls you 'A moron' and you are in a solid place of knowing and valuing self, you will in a kind and firm way return the verbal missive (missile!) to the person with the mature response, 'I'm wondering what makes you say that?' Because the person is more used to people reacting to his judgemental behaviour, he is likely to be surprised by the mature response and attempt to make light of or play down what he has said. The pity is that he misses an opportunity to explore the source of his verbal taunt and to discover what the behaviour is saying about himself. A possibility is that he feels 'small' within himself and any difference to what he feels, thinks, says and does touches (not causes, as Eleanor Roosevelt would have us believe) the raw nerve of what is already there within.

When you understand the behaviour of the person who uses a 'put down' as arising from his own internal sense of misery and inferiority, it follows that the person who is at the receiving end of the 'insulting' comment and who feels humiliated by the message also has an inner disconnection from his own true worth. It is a case of darkness meeting darkness, inferiority meeting inferiority and quiet desperation meeting quiet desperation. The person's aggressive reaction or physical and emotional withdrawal or self-harming responses are all protective ways of trying to ensure that the person does not attempt a 'putdown' again. What Eleanor Roosevelt needed to ask was: What is it that has led a person to perceive himself as inferior even *before* another person's derisive comment?

The answer to this question lies in the early years of that person's story when he experienced harsh criticism and emotional abandonment from a significant adult – parent, teacher, grandparent or childminder – and nobody championed his sacred worth in the face of those serious threats to his wellbeing. The frequency, intensity and endurance over time of these rejection experiences are important indices of the severity of the threats experienced.

Children are dependent on parents, childminders, grandparents and teachers to love, cherish, nurture, care, support, empower and play with them. They are not in a place to put food in their mouths, a roof over their heads and provide safety for themselves from physical, sexual, emotional, behavioural, intellectual and social threats to their wellbeing; on the contrary, they depend on the significant adults in their lives to do that. However, when parents and other adults become sources of threat, children, *unconsciously*, necessarily and creatively, develop protective responses in order to attempt to reduce the threats to their precious presence. A powerful protective response is to unconsciously 'take on' the critical messages and see oneself as described. This strategy means that a child who experiences constant criticism and is labelled as 'lazy' or 'no good' or 'a nuisance' or 'stupid' or 'slow' sensibly begins to perceive himself in the ways that the parent (or other adult) sees him, because it would be highly emotionally – even physically – threatening to protest that 'I am not any of the things you say of me; I am an individual and worthy of unconditional love.'

I am reminded of a woman in her mid-thirties telling me how she could not stop herself from doing 'bad' things – no matter how hard she tried. We discovered that her mother constantly told her that she was 'bad, bad, bad'. As an adult, when another adult labelled her as 'bad' it confirmed what she already felt about herself and she would either react aggressively or just avoid that person from thereon. This all happened unconsciously – she did not connect her present adult responses to her experiences as a child and the harsh rejection experienced from her mother. This failure to make the connection is clever because it means she stops herself from re-experiencing the misery of not being loved by the most important person in her life – her mother. Making the connection could only happen when she experienced – for the first time – an unconditional holding and deep and genuine cherishing of her presence; otherwise she would have needed to maintain her deep sense of inferiority and worthlessness.

Given the foregoing, we need to be sensitive about what comes from our mouths so that we are not reinforcing the inferiority felt by the many hurt individuals we meet. Each one of us has the opportunity to counter the rejections individuals have experienced by responding to each person with unconditional regard and enduring kindness. Remember – kindness is a two-way street!

Mis-taken Identity

In my recent book with co-author Helen Ruddle, *The Compassionate Intentions of Illness* (2010), I quote a passage from D.H. Lawrence on 'Healing':

> I am not a mechanism, an assembly of various sections.
> And it is not because the mechanism is working wrongly that I am ill.
> I am ill because of wounds to the soul, to the deep emotional self.
> And the wounds to the soul take a long, long time, only time can help.
> And patience, and a certain difficult repentance
> long difficult repentance, realization of life's mistake, and the freeing of oneself
> from the endless repetition of the mistake
> which mankind at large has chosen to sanctify.

What does Lawrence mean by the word 'mistake' and the sanctification of that mistake? My own interpretation is that the mistake – best written mis-take – refers to how from so early on in our lives we are mistaken for our particular qualities or behaviours, and how this confusion of our soul, our true emotional self, with such phenomena results in deep wounds to the unique self that is each one of us.

Whether the mis-take is about 'good' or 'bad' qualities or behaviours, a great darkness descends on us and, until some time in adulthood when we have the time and safety to examine the mistake, we are compelled to create protectors to reduce the threats that the mistakes pose. The most common mis-take is that a person is their behaviour and from that confusion arises such judgements as 'you're a difficult person', 'you're a bully', 'you're a bold boy', 'you're a clever kid', 'you're a good girl'. Much more harsh judgements are 'you're bad', 'sad', 'mad', 'insane', 'selfish', ' neurotic', 'psychotic', 'lazy', 'no-good', 'depressive', 'a waste of space'. What is often not appreciated is that the person who is told that she is 'so good' or 'so clever' is as much threatened as the person who is told that they are 'bad', 'impossible' and so on. Suicide is a common phenomenon around examination times and arises from fears of falling short of the perceived unrealistic expectations and falling off the pedestal that the person has been put upon. Similarly, individuals who are perfectionistic in their behaviours believe that any mistake will result in rejection by the person who has mistaken them for getting things right all of the time; as a consequence they will strive relentlessly to be perfect. The 'realization of life's mistake' that is required for this person is that 'I'm not my behaviour, perfection lies in my unique being and presence, and mistakes and failures are wonderful opportunities to learn more about the world.' The latter process takes a long, long time because the person's intense endeavours to be perfect have been 'sanctified' over and over again within her home, classrooms and workplaces. Nobody corrected the mis-take and affirmed the person for her unique presence and demonstrated that behaviour is a means of understanding and exploring our inner and outer worlds; it is not a means of proving myself and it certainly is not the self.

Arising from their earlier childhood experiences, many men believe (mistakenly) that they are their achievement and a high percentage of them become depressed when they experience career failure. Sadly, these men's addiction to success would have resulted in poor marital relationships, strained relationships with their children and the endless repetition of the mistake in their daily work life. Work is a wonderful expression of the immense power of our nature but I am not my work achievements and that realisation means I can enjoy my work in a way that I don't live to work but I do work to live. Work organisations believe that those addicted to success – highly engaged – are a great asset (thereby sanctifying the mistake), but the reality is that they are a great threat to the well-being of others and are not mature and effective managers.

What does Lawrence mean by the 'soul, the deep emotional self'? Intuitively, we have a sense of ourselves as being unique, as being unlike any other, a distinctiveness that cannot be pinned down to anything tangible, such as particular dimensions of our physical appearance, or a particular type of intelligence, or a particular way of believing, or a particular way of relating, or a particular way of feeling. The self as unique presence has a physical mirror in the uniqueness of my DNA, and more observably in my fingerprints. My self is unrepeatable and, as a unique presence, as inviolate wholeness, is present from the moment of conception. There is no greater wounding to the self, to the soul, than to mistake the self for how we look, what we feel, think, say and do. The redemption of the self from the endless repetition of the mistake is our most urgent responsibility.

A Person Always Knows What's Going On

I just want to address an unspoken secret – each individual understands precisely what makes him or her do what they do! This runs contrary to what many people believe – including some psychoanalysts and psychotherapists. The belief is that people lack awareness or lack insight or need to understand what underlies their behaviour – anxiety, depression, illness, delusion, illusion, violence, whatever. The experts believe that their job is to provide the person with insights into their behaviour or to bring them to awareness of what made them act in ways that are threatening to themselves or to others. There are also many parents and teachers who feel they know what is best for children and young people and, accordingly, provide advice, whether or not requested. The difficulty with such superiority – that 'I know what's best for you' or 'I can understand you better than you can understand yourself' – is that it shows no belief in the person addressed and fails to mirror the understanding that is present within that person. Advice-giving and providing awareness also blocks the person from examining their own interiority and finding their own answers. Furthermore, the answers provided by others may be totally off the mark of what is really going on for the other person. In any case, solutions provided by any expert are all about the expert and his or her present level of maturity. It is far more mature to provide the unconditional loving and safe environment necessary for the person to access their own understanding and determine their own solutions.

A pertinent question here is: how can you say somebody always know what's going on for him (or her)? Surely, for example, a male partner that is violent towards his female partner can hardly be seen to understand what drives him to such a violent means of control! The answer is that understanding lies at an *unconscious* level. The man who is being aggressive creates his defensive responses in order to protect himself from abandonment; the purpose of his violence is to ensure his partner does not leave him or reject him. His experience as a child would have been that his individual presence did not spontaneously gain unconditional love and approval. In the face of such abandonment he cleverly creates an alternative and substitute means of having his wholeness held – aggression, a forcing of another to be there for him. All of these defensive responses are created by him – albeit unconsciously – but nevertheless he *knows* at that unconscious level that he had to develop these responses in order to survive the experiences of abandonment. Surely it makes sense that when the person unconsciously creates the defence, he knows exactly why he is doing it. However, he needs to keep that knowing and understanding *below* consciousness, because it would be far too painful to live with the every moment consciousness of harsh abandonment.

In helping a person in distress, the realisation that the person understands is paramount. The intention of helping the person would be to create the unconditional loving environment and physical, emotional, intellectual and social safety for the understanding that is below the surface to rise up into consciousness. I recall working with a man who, in his own words, treated his son 'like shit'. When safety was established I asked him, 'What do you feel leads you to be so harsh with your son?' The answer was spontaneous: 'Because I see myself as a lump of shit.'

It is very powerful and liberating when individuals in turmoil realise and understand the sources of their threatening behaviours. It is both an act of unconditional love and belief in them when we communicate that 'I have no doubt that you have a deep inner understanding of what makes you act in the ways you do'. When this understanding rises to consciousness the person feels strongly motivated to change the nature of his relationship with self and with others. Great patience is required, because when an individual has been deeply hurt he is very slow to again take the risk of reaching out and responding in an authentic, real and spontaneous way. Sometimes it can take years of patience and the provision of unconditional love before the person is willing to trust again. There is a wonderful anonymous saying that encourages patience: 'I will wait patiently, even for an eternity, for you to become present to your precious life.'

Uncovering the Intentions of Stress

I gave my first talk on 'Coping with Stress' back in 1982 in An Grianán, Termonfeckin, Co. Louth. How I viewed stress back then is very different to how I now see it. However, in reading several recent articles on the subject, I find that the advice I gave back in 1982 has not changed. Suggestions around work–life balance, relaxation skills, healthy diet and physical exercise continue to dominate

the stress literature. As regards the popular work–life balance recommendation, I find this notion confusing as it suggests that work is
not an integral part of living and that living can only be enjoyed
when you are not working! In my opinion, work is an integral part of
my living and this view is reflected very powerfully and poetically by
Khalil Gibran, when he says, 'Work is love made visible.' I would
put it somewhat differently: 'Work (potentially) is your Real Self
made visible.' However, sadly, not too many individuals operate out
from that solid interiority and it is too often the case that 'work is fear
made visible' and, inevitably, becomes stressful in nature.

How do I view stress now? In the past, I would have responded
to stress symptoms – for example, rushing, racing, worrying, being
aggressive, perfectionistic, fear of failure, long working hours,
success addiction – as behaviours that needed to be reduced and
eventually eliminated. The difficulty with this approach is that it is
critical of the symptoms presented, rather than realising that a
symptom *always* signals something deeper that is calling for attention – this is as true for medicine and psychiatry as it is for
psychology and sociology. Human beings have the remarkable
unconscious ability to bring attention to what they dare not express
consciously but can express in symbolic ways. For example, in my
own life I used to suffer from excruciating and crippling lower back
pain. Lower back pain is the most common stress symptom and
accounts for a high percentage of absenteeism from work. For
several years, I responded to my back pain in a literal and critical
way. In other words, I looked on my back pain as a problem to be
gotten rid of rather than a symptom to be understood. I followed a
lot of advice I used to give to clients – rest, relaxation, physical
fitness, work–life balance. These interventions certainly eased the
pain but never addressed the deeper issue. Inevitably, the pain
returned – and this is the wisdom of a symptom to keep recurring
until the hidden issue is addressed. I partially addressed the hidden
issue with the realisation that I took too much responsibility for
others on my back but it took me longer to realise that the deepest
issue was that I constantly 'turned (twisted) my back on any care for

my self'. This realisation was the 'turning point', and taking action on more care for myself has eliminated the incapacitating pain. I still get an odd twinge but I am quick to respond to the signal and return to care for self.

Stress is then best seen metaphorically as 'pointing to' or 'emphasising' a hidden, unconscious issue that requires resolution. The hidden issue has always to do with some troubling aspect of your relationship with self that is not in your consciousness. For example, many men have come to me for help complaining of 'being all stressed out' from the demands of their jobs. They come looking for ways of managing the stressful situation and are surprised by the deeper exploration of the possible absence of work on their own relationship with self. Indeed, the hardest work for men to take on is to find heart for themselves – to nurture and take care of themselves – and to consciously realise 'I am not my work.' The resolution for many men's stress at work is to reclaim their own self-worthiness and to actively ensure that their own wellbeing and the wellbeing of their intimate relationships with others and with their children are not jeopardised by work demands. They need to inhabit their own individuality and to assert their own values and, particularly, that people matter infinitely more than profits and success. Ironically, the mature employee, manager and employer is far more creative and productive, but this is a bridge too far for many men who, dependently, get their recognition through work and success.

What about the most stressed member of our society – the married woman, with children and career – what is the hidden issue there? Many women have a major difficulty in asking for and receiving help and are not conscious of how unworthy they feel to receive. Resolution of their stress involves becoming conscious of their unconscious fear of asking and receiving, being compassionate towards their neglect of themselves and beginning to make the authentic choice to start saving themselves and allow others to save themselves. Love, of its very nature, is about giving and receiving. The receiving of love and care is as much a privilege as the giving of love and care.

Stressing the Not So Obvious

The word stress is typically described as pressure and the idea is that you look at the external or internal (or both) circumstances of your life and detect what aspects are leading to your being all stressed out. Frequently individuals may point the finger at work, financial pressures, marriage, children and family of origin or living next door to the neighbour from hell. There are some people who don't even look that far and what they attempt to do is find orthodox medical or alternative means of reducing the stress symptoms. The more common symptoms people focus on are tension headaches, migraine, back pain, chest pain, increased heart rate, high blood pressure, dizziness, excessive perspiration, dryness of the mouth, insomnia, trembling, depression, fatigue and nervousness. Possible remedies pursued are drug taking, meditation, relaxation exercises, time-management.

Those people who choose to examine the internal circumstances of their lives may detect any number of the following symptoms: anxiety, fear, depression, worry about the future, regrets about the past, fear of failure, addiction to success, fear of illness, suppressed anger, hypersensitivity to criticism and mental blocks. The response to these stress signs may be to seek out counselling and/or resort to tranquilisers, anti-depressants or any combination of these 'cures'.

The difficulty with seeing the external or internal signs of stress as the problems to be resolved is that the true purpose of the stress symptoms are not being detected or acted upon. After all, the word 'symptom' means a 'sign', an indicator that there is some *underlying hidden* issue that needs to be addressed. In physical medicine a persistent pain to the right of your lower abdomen may indicate a threatened appendicitis, or a recurring abdominal pain may point to a duodenal ulcer. However, when it comes to stress symptoms, the true nature of the word symptom appears to get lost. The purpose of an internal or external stress symptom is to *emphasise* some aspect of the self that is being neglected and the response needed is to directly address this self-issue and not the symptom itself. All the latter will do is reduce or extinguish the very important information about the self to which the symptom is attempting to draw attention. In any case, symptomatic treatment will not resolve the core issue and, inevitably, either the symptom will flare up again or some new, more serious symptom will appear.

Take the most common stress symptom occurring at this moment in time, namely exam stress. There are several psychological, alternative and medical 'cures' given for this symptom – counselling to reduce fear of failure, positive thinking, reflexology, meditation or tranquilisers. However, exam stress actually has nothing to do with worry about exams! At face value you might rightly say that this is what the young (or older) person is saying: 'I'm really worried about my exams.' However, this symptom is masking the real issue that needs urgent attending to and that is, 'I am not an exam result.' When a person feels that an exam result is a measure of their self-worth, then it is the self issue that needs to be resolved. When a young person can be helped to see and feel that her worth lies in her unique and sacred presence and that an examination is a very limited test of knowledge of the test set that does not in any way measure her worth, then examination stress dissolves. I have no difficulty with individuals pursuing the various means described above of reducing their symptoms, but I do want to let them know that resolution of the stress symptom will only come about when the threat to self acceptance has been removed.

In my experience, anxiety is not really about what other people think about us, even though ostensibly this may seem to be the case. What anxiety is truly about is the fear or terror of showing some aspects of self – spontaneity, expression of feelings such as anger, disappointment, love, risk-taking, speaking the truth. Visualise yourself being totally true to self, in possession of self, feeling a rock-hard sense of self, fully aware of your own immense power to take responsibility for your own life – will you feel continually anxious? Hardly!

The other most common internal symptom – depression – attempts to bring attention to the aspects of self that are suppressed, buried, flattened, deeply hidden. Examples are: your lovability, uniqueness, difference, creativity, anger, worthiness, right to live your own life. The stress symptom of depression attempts to *emphasise* those hidden qualities of self and invites the person to detect and begin to express them. Once again, visualise yourself seeing your immense lovability, specialness, difference and feeling the extent of living from the inside out, feeling free and empowered. Will you now feel depressed? Of course not!

Stress, then, is an ally, a friend, who sends you an invitation to dig deep and discover what aspect(s) of self need to be recovered so that you find yourself back on a wellbeing path.

The Intelligence of Stress

Angela Patmore, author, who served in the Metropolitan Police External Experts Stress Advisory Group, claims 'there really is no such thing as stress' (Patmore, 2009). Indeed, she goes on to say that 'stress is a mythical malaise – a designer disease'. Does this mean that when a mother is stressed out from the constant wailing of a baby, or an employee is bullied daily in the workplace, or a person is stressed out from overworking, rushing and racing or a woman is terrified because she might have breast cancer, that all of these stress responses are imaginary, not real? And the many men who take their lives because of deep inner turmoil, is Patmore saying this is not real?

Admittedly, stress is a relatively new word for human distress and turmoil. Interestingly, the word was borrowed from science, which recognises that when prolonged and extended pressure is put on metal, it fatigues and breaks down. Several plane crashes have been known to be due to metal fatigue: too much strain and pressure put on the metal over too long a period of time.

The word stress means pressure and strain and is a much kinder word than the older descriptions of human distress: 'she's suffering from her nerves', 'he's neurotic or psychotic' or 'your man is a bit peculiar'. Use of the word stress has not created more human problems, as Patmore would have us believe, but it has made it easier for people to more readily identify such problems. In the area of psychosomatic medicine it is well documented that the six leading causes of death – heart disease, cancer, cirrhosis of the liver, lung ailments, accidents and suicide – are either directly or indirectly caused by stress. General practitioners admit that up to seventy per cent of visits to them are due to stress-related difficulties (Charlesworth and Nathan, 1987). I believe Patmore misses the point when she describes stress as 'a designer disease' and is closer to the point when she claims that 'stress is a perfectly normal emotion with normal physiological reactions'.

In claiming that it is a 'designer disease', she slips into the very thing she warns us not to do – she *medicalises* stress symptoms. I totally agree that stress be not medicalised, but in calling it a disease she is not seeing the true purpose of stress. In saying it is a normal emotion that signals the need for action, she is closer to the truth of what stress is all about. What she fails to point out is that it is not stress that poses the threat to our wellbeing, but the *not acting* on it. It is wiser to view the stress response metaphorically and view it as attempting to *bring emphasis* to some aspect of a person's internal and/or external life that needs resolution. Stress is an ally, a friend that is calling out for a person to take whatever actions are needed to restore a sense of being in charge and a sense of equilibrium. When a person denies, ignores, dismisses the signs and the effects of stress, the risks to their health increase because they are not taking responsibility for the conflicts in their lives. Of its very nature, the stress response, the normal emotional and physiological responses, will increase in intensity to wake the person up to the urgent need to set about resolving their inner and outer conflicts. Rather than debunking stress, it would better serve people if Patmore were to help individuals see the intelligence of the stress response in its creative attempt to bring attention to what needs attending. Stress will arise as the SOS signaller in the area where conflicts are occurring – family, marriage, work, community, Church and, most of all, self. The specific stress symptom is designed to emphasise the particular conflict that needs resolution.

For example, back pain may indicate that the person afflicted is 'taking too much on his back' or that 'his back is against the wall' or that 'he easily gets his back up at work' or that he feels he has 'no back-up'. A tension headache may be drawing attention to 'wanting to be always a-head' or 'too much going on in one's head' or a situation that the person feels that they 'are banging their head off a stone wall'.

In my experience, all human behaviour makes sense, and what people need is the support, the encouragement and the conflict-resolution skills to respond to the intelligent manifestation of stress response in their daily lives. Stress calls for action to bring about wellbeing; it is an essential and wise mechanism.

The Heart of the Matter

Over the last two decades there have been many amazing medical advances and one of the multinational success stories has been the development of technological aids in the medical treatments of cardiovascular disease – for example pacemakers, stents, cardiac balloons. The statistics on heart disease are frightening. Heart disease is the greatest killer of human life, but then why are we surprised by that when we consider how the heart has been 'killed off' in a high proportion of relationships within marriage, family, community, classrooms, sports clubs and workplaces. The emergence of HR (human resources) departments and their replacement of Personnel Departments give some indication of how products and profits became more important than people. It is vital to see that the development of such 'heart-less' organisations rests on the shoulders of entrepreneurs who themselves had suspended having heart for self and others and taken on the substitute goals of work and success as means of gaining recognition. The irony of it is that individuals who are self-reliant are more creative and productive than those who rely on substitutes. It is the wise work organisation (a collective of individuals) that recognises that their most important asset is the individual mature employee and that his or her wellbeing cannot afford to be jeopardised by unrealistic targets, deadlines and unrelenting pressures to perform.

Pacemakers, stents and cardiac balloons are technological substitutes for what individuals have not been doing for themselves. The stent offers support to a heart that is collapsing, a pacemaker is designed to create a healthy heart rhythm and the cardiac balloon inflates the blocked arteries. These technological creations carry out the responsibilities that the individuals afflicted have not been in a safe enough place to do for themselves. It is no coincidence that it is men who are far more likely to develop heart disease; after all, men's hearts can be constantly under attack from the neglect they perpetrate around love and kindness towards self and others and the expression of their emotions. Emotions call for motions – movements – to be made, actions for self that need to be taken, depending on the particular emergency feeling that has arisen – fear, anger, depression, sadness, guilt, loneliness, humiliation. When men fail to act on their feelings and are not 'heartfelt' in their relationship with self and others, then those emotional blocks become creatively embodied in cardiac symptoms. When these physical manifestations do not result in 'a change of heart' then the possibility of the ultimate creation arises – the heart attack. Metaphorically, the huge numbers of bypass heart operations powerfully represent how often men bypass their hearts. Georg Groddeck, the founder of psychosomatic medicine, believed that 'when a person is alienated from the self the last act of creation may be an illness' (Groddeck, 1977).

The development of many illnesses arises in individuals living in a substitute world, rather than in the real world of individual and unique self-expression. The most common substitute for men is work. Many men believe that they *are* their work. When they were children they learned that their worth lay not in their unique presence, but in what they did. A high percentage of men die quite soon after retiring from work, even though there was no sign of disease present at the time of retiring. Of course, many men do not reach retirement age. Those who do, complain that they 'have nothing left to live for'. What an emotional and spiritual desert that is. Often, the substitute for recognition that precedes employment is an examination result. Children as young as six years complain of being 'all stressed out by tests'. This experience runs contrary to the excitement of the toddler, who loves tests and risk-taking! The difference is in how seriously adults – parents, teachers, neighbours and relatives – view examination results. I have worked with many parents who were obsessed with their children's school progress and missed detecting the considerable emotional turmoil that their children were undergoing. This blindness on the part of parents and others is an unconscious creation and support to their own addictions (substitutes) to success or what others think. No parent or teacher wants to intentionally block a child's progress, but the reality is that unless, as adults, we resolve our own substitute ways and live from the inside out rather than from the outside in, we are not in a place to unconditionally love children.

Recent research in Ireland has shown that we are undergoing an epidemic of stress disorders, and drug companies are determined to develop new drugs that will more effectively control the brain mechanisms that can be overactivated due to individuals putting themselves under pressure. At a time when we are experiencing an unprecedented reliance on illicit drugs (another substitute), it is sadly ironic that there is a push to develop more legal drugs that will do for us what we need to do for ourselves. I cannot for the life of me see the difference between being addicted to a legal or illegal drug as a substitute for filling the void within. We need researchers and health professionals who are committed to the *real* wellbeing of individuals and whose findings will direct us down the road of living from the inside out and being self-reliant within all the human systems we inhabit.

The Truth in the Lie

We were brought up with the Catholic notion that 'a lie is always sinful'. Recently I was sitting alone in a favourite restaurant of mine in Greece and while waiting for wine and food I began to mull over the matter of lying. The thought that arose was 'a lie is always truthful'. I put the line into my mobile phone and at one point showed it to a young Iranian waiter who knew me from previous visits and asked, 'What do you think of that?' He read it, smiled and responded, 'I'll have to think about that.' Later, he returned to me and said, 'Had you realised that on several occasions in the past I have been drunk when I served you?' He went on to tell me that he drank at least a half bottle of whiskey a day, but lied when his wife or anyone else questioned him about his drinking. I asked him, 'What is the truth in your lie?' He promptly replied, 'Loneliness'. It transpired his wife worked from 9 a.m. to 5 p.m. and he worked six days from 5 p.m. to 1 a.m. They only met one day a week. I enquired, 'What makes it difficult for you to admit to your wife your loneliness?' Like many men, he saw it as a weakness to talk about his emotions and the lie of 'bottling up' (literally and metaphorically) the truth was the preferable option. This has relevance to my clinical experience of third-level students who experience depression but most of them put 'a brave face' on it (lie). They feel that nobody would understand their depression. This does not surprise me, particularly when medical professionals persist in the notion that depression is an illness rather than a healthy manifestation of inner turmoil that requires resolution. Even the World Health Organisation reinforces this misinterpretation of depression by estimating that 'depressive illness will be ranked as the second most disabling medical disorder by 2020'. Depression is *not* a medical disorder; it in an *ordered* response to psychological turmoil within the person and social stressors outside the person. Neither is depression due to what has been popularly called 'negative thoughts' or 'negative internal commentary'. This internal dialogue has the important purpose of protecting the person from further experiences of hurt. If depression is not a medical condition, neither is it a cognitive disorder. In my experience, depression is about relationship – relationship with self and with others. There is no doubt that a person's poor sense of self lies at the heart of depression, but this low self-esteem can be exacerbated by external factors. Outside factors can be bullying, poor college-relationship ethos, pressure to succeed, isolation from peers, difficulties in intimate relationships and financial strains. However, the student who has a strong sense of self will automatically seek support when these challenges arise. The student who feels inferior will respond to these crises as further convincing evidence of his worthlessness and is likely to plummet into depression and suicidal ideation. The threat is *not* the depression and the suicidal thoughts; the threat lies deeper – the reality that the young person is cut off from any sense of his worth and value. Depression and suicidal thoughts and words mirror the inner disconnection from self and are attempts to 'wake up' the person himself, and others who encounter him, to his unhappy plight. Labelling and dire predictions are not helpful responses. Love, understanding, belief in, support, patience and encouragement are much-needed responses.

When a supportive environment is created, young people do not need to 'lie' about how they are feeling; when a supportive environment is not present the 'lies' ('I'm o.k.', 'I'm fine', 'no worries, that's me') are necessary because the threats of judgement, being labelled, medicated and misunderstood are the last thing the young person wants to encounter. The truth in the lie is that 'it is not safe for me to say what is happening to me; it is safer to hide the truth behind the lie'.

Mind Without Heart is Not Mind At All

The word 'mind' is generally defined as what goes on in your head – thoughts, imaginings, inventions, problem-solving, analysis, planning, dreams, post-mortems, self-criticism, judgements, appraisals, memories. When individuals miss the fact that the word 'mind' also means 'to care for', then such mind without heart is not mind at all! In other words, when the heart qualities of love, tenderness, nurture, empathy, support, comfort, warmth and affection are not present, the head without the heart can prove to be rigid, judgemental, controlling, inflexible, arrogant, depersonalising, superior, dismissive and intolerant. Our human nature only achieves equilibrium when the polarities of head and heart, feminine and masculine and right-brain and left-brain are in harmony with each other. When the head, which is largely about 'getting ahead' – an outward movement – is not balanced by the inward movement of the heart, it can rule in a heartless way and be a major source of threat to the wellbeing of others. For example, the man who is highly ambitious – success being his God – will neglect his relationship with his wife and children, resulting in considerable trauma for them. In the workplace, the loss of his own valuing of himself will manifest in a depersonalising of other staff members and clients. While he does this unconsciously from a deep insecurity and a need to be visible through success, the reality is that his head without heart for himself, his partner, children and employees results in threats to his own wellbeing and that of the significant others in his life. I recall one businessman saying to me that when colleagues warned him that his intense working schedule would give him a heart attack, his response was, 'I won't get a heart attack; I'm the one who gives heart attacks.' The emotional disconnection evident in this stark and harsh assertion 'I give heart attacks' shows very clearly the major danger posed by a mind without heart. Incidentally – and sadly – three years later he suffered a heart attack – hence his seeking psychotherapeutic help recommended by an astute medical general practitioner. Sometimes it takes a major psychological crisis or illness to bring about a consciousness of hidden vulnerabilities that need resolution.

What is often not appreciated is that if mind without heart is a considerable threat to wellbeing, heart without mind is also darkness within and between people. The person who over-involves themselves in the life of another (for example, mother with child, friend with friend, wife with husband, employee with employer) is without mind. If mind – understanding, outwardness, determination, ambition, intention, assertion – were present then the over-belonging would be perceived as a dependence on the other, a living one's life for the other and, thereby, making it difficult – particularly for a child – to live his or her own life. Indeed, many intimate couple relationships are troubled due to an over-involved partner living her life through her partner, or the opposite scenario – under-involvement – is common, whereby one partner jealously possesses, dominates and blocks any bid for independence on the part of his partner. Similar over- and under-involvement can occur in the workplace. I have helped individuals who bent themselves over backwards for their employers – living their lives for them – only to be devastated when criticised or, worse still, made redundant. Basically, such over-involvement with another is saying, 'I should be there for you and live my life for you.' If you are in a conscious place right now just imagine how imprisoning this liaison is, unless, of course, the object of the defensive relationship rebels or asserts that 'this is far too claustrophobic'. The under-involvement situation captured in the phrase 'you should be there for me and live your life for me' is equally terrifying. Individuals who tend to be passive are more likely to live for others and those who bully and are aggressive demand 'others live for them'; either way it is not a mature and happy situation. Individuals then who are over- or under-involved and enmeshed with another are in an unconscious state of denial and unless they become mindful – conscious with heart – of their dependence on the other, then their own maturity is seriously blocked. This unhappy situation has its origins in childhood – in the key relationship between a parent and a child. For mindfulness to emerge, the person who is enmeshed needs to encounter somebody who stays separate from her or him and provides the unconditional holding that creates the support for the crucial engagement with self and disengagement from another that is required. Without such support, it is unlikely that heart with mindfulness will emerge.

Each Person is a Genius!

One of the best kept secrets is that 'each person is a genius'. Even though this secret has been confirmed by science, it is remarkable the degree to which the vast majority of individuals still hide away their limitless intelligence. Of course, it is ingenious to hide the light of your intelligence 'under a bushel' because to assert 'I'm a genius' is likely to be greeted with ridicule, laughter, judgement and criticism – a fate worse than death!

Children become secure through the mirroring of their genius. However, when other adults who have responsibility for the care and education of children have creatively colluded with the secret, then it would be too threatening for them to affirm their child's genius; they rightly fear that their child would also be subjected to ridicule. The result is that the best kept secret continues and, alongside adults, children struggle with actively believing in their power beyond measure.

One of the creative confusions that emerged around intelligence and led to learning and work becoming threats to a person's well-being is that knowledge is a measure of intelligence. Typically, children who demonstrate a high knowledge of the three R's – reading, writing and arithmetic – are rated and labelled as being 'bright' or 'superior' or 'genius'. This confusion creates an addiction to high marks and success, and suicide is not an untypical response to a failure to meet such high expectations.

Knowledge is an index of learning and the readiness and motivation to learn specific subjects is determined by a multiplicity of variables, most importantly emotional security and interest. Emotional security arises principally from unconditional love – a deep loving, celebration and cherishing of the unique presence of the individual person, whether child or adult. Unconditional love recognises the unique self that each person is and does not confuse the self with any of its expressions, including intelligence; neither does unconditional love confuse the self with any behaviour – academic, athletic, musical, creative, occupational, emotional or social.

Once a person is confused with a particular self-expression, then an addiction to or an avoidance or a rebelliousness will arise in response to that expression. For example, approximately eighty per cent of students go for the average – a reality that makes teaching very challenging; a reality too that has serious outcomes for society in terms of disengagement from work and the avoidance of risk-taking and dynamic creativity and productivity. Going for the average is an avoidance strategy that involves making minimum efforts and achieving average attainments so that the expectations of parents, teachers and employers are reduced from high to average to low. The wonder is that this strategy is *ingenious* because it reduces or eliminates the greatest threat to a person's wellbeing – emotional rejection.

Children and adults are *not* a reservoir of a particular knowledge field, or a particular skill or talent, or an examination result or an academic degree or anything that they do, say, feel or think. Classrooms and workplaces would be far more proactive and adventurous places if the unique presence of each member was cherished and where there was an active recognition of the genius that each person possesses. However, until those who manage and are leaders of those four critical social systems – the family, the school, the workplace, the church – redeem their own unique sense of self and their unique power beyond measure, due to the immense dangers of rejection, ridicule and humiliation, it is unlikely that young people will dare raise their heads above the parapet of mediocrity. In these times of recession, it has become critical that the powerful emotional processes that underlay the major economic downturn be addressed. Major aspects of these emotional processes are, one, a confusion of self with what an individual does, resulting in either a fear of failure or an addiction to success and, two, the depersonalisation, disempowering and de-individualising of individuals within homes, schools, workplaces and churches. Recessions offer glorious opportunities for reflection, particularly on the issue of man's protective inhumanity to self and man's inhumanity to man.

Is There More To Your Career Than You Realise?

Does the career we have chosen have a much deeper purpose than the pursuit of our work goals? After all, when we think that our most important work of all is to know ourselves and to cut the ties that bind us to past and present relationships, is it possibly a reality that our career choice carries a deeper message regarding our unconscious drive to be true to ourselves? The self is ingenious in the ways it attempts to draw attention to the unresolved conflicts that continue to block our progress within ourselves and between ourselves and others. The obvious way the self does this is by attracting into one's life people who manifest opposite qualities to oneself, and it is the case that these qualities are the very ones to date that one dare not express or confront.

Over the years I have found, for example, that some people who enter the army or police forces are highly defended in their relationships with others and their sense of self lies hidden behind their defensive walls. Their childhood experiences were of a nature where they had to constantly be 'on guard' against physical, emotional and, sometimes, sexual blows to their presence. The fact that they enter the defence forces reinforces their subconscious ways of defending themselves against the 'slings and arrows of outrageous misfortune', but it also powerfully draws their attention to the urgent need for them to free themselves of how others see and relate to them. Such a process depends on real and authentic outside support and the person creating a safe environment within themselves and strong boundaries (not defences) around care for themselves.

I have also come across individuals who enter professions where they are constantly involved in the caring of neglected children. What these individuals had not seen was that their chosen profession daily brought them back to the childhood neglects they had experienced themselves and to their failure over time to grieve and resolve these profound abandonments.

Covering up our feelings of hurt and rejection is a common defensive manoeuvre and there are several professions that mirror and reinforce that deeper process, the most obvious being cosmetics, beauty therapy and fashion design. The deeper and underlying issue is the 'covering up' or the 'dressing up' of the 'ugliness' of being rejected, compared, labelled and not cherished for your own true and beautiful self. The 'uncovering' of one's true self is what is being called for.

Of course, the phrase 'physician heal yourself' strongly gives credence to the notion that a chosen career may be attempting to unearth unresolved conflicts. Medicine is the most 'at-risk' profession in terms of life expectancy, health, marriage and family relationships. The indicators are that the person who enters a 'healing' profession may need to do considerable healing of old and present emotional wounds. When the reading between the lines of their chosen career path is done, medical professionals can deepen their capacity to help others from the experience of healing their own insecurities and hurts. When this path less travelled is *not* taken, there is a danger that their dedication to others becomes counterproductive, certainly escalating the threat to their own wellbeing and, sometimes, to those people who attend them.

There are many of us who need to 'dig deep' or explore our inner lives in order to resolve the long-term blocks to a fulfilling and exciting life. There are those individuals who choose interior design or architecture or archaeology as career paths. It may well be that the interior designer needs to discover the colour, breadth and light of her own interiority and that the architect needs to become the architect of his own inner world. The archaeologist subconsciously may be called to dig deep into his sense of self and explore the ruins of his early experiences. People who are fearful of knowing oneself often warn others to 'not go so deep' as if somehow there is some border of knowing one should not cross! On the contrary, when we do not reflect on who we are, what living is all about and how we are in relationships, there is a great danger that we will repeat in some way or other the neglect of self and the neglect of others. Typically, when I work with individuals in deep distress, I can trace back the origins of their difficulties six and seven generations. This is not a genetic phenomenon, but a situation where reflection on and resolution of conflict have not occurred across the generations. It is no wonder that the psyche (the self) uses every possible opportunity to waken individuals up to the sacred reality of their unique lives and I believe the work we do is one of the canvasses used to project onto and awaken us to the darkness of our pasts.

I can't finish without mentioning my own work – clinical psychology. Psychology is now the highest-sought third-level and postgraduate subject. Psychology is the study of the self (the psyche) and as regards myself, I have no doubt that what attracted me to a career in clinical psychology was the dire need for me to reclaim my lost sense of self. If I had not realised the *deeper* call that my job called on me to do, I believe I would not be near as mature as I am. All the evidence points to the fact that the greater the level of personal maturity of a therapeutic practitioner the greater is his or her effectiveness. There is more to most behaviour than meets the conscious eye or ear!

After All, It's Only Human To . . .

'It is only human' is a phrase that I frequently come upon either as an explanation for or a verbal response to expressed anger, loss of temper, irritability, failure and forgetfulness. It is the 'only' that triggers something that is already in me, in that I perceive it as a diminishment of what it means to be 'truly' human. Somehow, too, the 'only human' I perceive as a clever way to reduce the weight and impact of another's particular actions, especially those that create an unsafe situation for another person – adult or child – to be in our company. Furthermore, the 'only human' response suggests that such threatening actions are 'beyond our control' and absolves us of having to reflect on and resolve the causes and intentions of these responses.

The reality is that as human we are highly intelligent and even the use of the term 'only human' arises paradoxically from that power. When human beings are under physical, sexual, emotional and intellectual threats they find the most amazing ways of reducing or eliminating such threats. We have developed the most sophisticated technology to safeguard our homes, property and our own physical wellbeing. Equally, when we encounter 'put downs', irritability, dismissal and aggression we find creative and powerful ways to offset the threats by blaming the perpetrators or by becoming 'martyrs' to these responses. In blaming, we put all the responsibility for our feelings of hurt, disappointment, devastation onto the other; in being passive and 'martyred' we attempt to offset further 'blows' by blaming ourselves and by 'keeping a low profile' or by inviting the sympathy of others in the hope that they might champion us against further hurts. Whatever the response, it is clever, creative and powerful and hardly 'only human'.

In considering our responses to the difficult behaviours of others, it helps to understand that their actions are their creative and powerful attempts to offset threats to their wellbeing. For example, when somebody is dismissive of your sacred presence, it certainly indicates that that person is protectively unsure of self and in some way or another perceives your presence or behaviour as a threat. What is assuredly true is that if that person possessed a solid sense of self, he or she would be affirming of your presence. The responsibility for the threatening behaviour of another is completely theirs and does not arise from your presence or behaviour but from that person's own interiority. Equally, our responses to the threatening behaviours of others belong to us and are not caused by their hostile behaviours but arise from our own interiority. It is for that reason when you encounter a response that is demeaning and lessening of your presence that you take action *for yourself* to hold true to your own self and return or leave the defensive response with the person who has engaged in it. However, when we are not operating from an inner stronghold of self, we will wisely 'personalise' the other person's demeaning behaviour because it is too threatening to speak the truth. 'Personalising' results in us either protectively 'acting in' (passive, blaming self) or 'acting-out' (aggressive, blaming others), but its deeper purpose is to awaken us, when it is emotionally safe for us to do so, to honour our own person ('personal-ise' self) and stay separate from the dark actions of others.

Whether we are at the receiving end and personalising or are perpetrating actions that lessen others' presence, the underlying issue is our particular sense of self that is present at that moment in time.

'Blows' (the protective responses of others) to our presence occur in all social systems – home, school, community, workplace and church. How we respond to these 'blows' depends on several things:

- our level of self-esteem at the time
- the frequency, intensity and endurance of the 'blows'
- our state of physical and psychosocial wellbeing.

One's level of self-esteem can change from time to time, person to person and situation to situation. At 'crisis' times it can be challenging to hold strongly to our incredible worth and capability, while at times of celebration, such holding is easier. When it comes to people, with certain people who are caring and respectful of us, to 'feel good about ourselves' can arise effortlessly, but when we encounter 'authority' figures we can often find ourselves 'feeling small' in their company. There is also the reality that no matter how strong a hold of self you possess, when you encounter frequently intense and daily and long-enduring years of 'blows' to your presence, it can be extremely difficult to not personalise. Similarly, when our energy is low, or we're acutely or chronically ill, or experiencing serious marital or familial or work-related problems, the challenge to stay centred, solid and separate is difficult. There is the fact too that we are not surrounded by individuals who strongly practise self-realisation. What is far more common is what I call 'lean to' relationships. It is from such vulnerable relationships that the response 'it is *only* human' arises.

2 Men on Top

Men on Top

What has been evident since the economic crash is that it was men who peopled the 'top' positions in the banks, financial institutions and property development companies. Men at the top are also a feature of the front bench (and the back benches) of the present government and of the opposition parties. Of course, this phenomenon of male predominance is blaringly apparent in the Catholic Church. What is now clear is that these male leaders have not done a good job – cover ups, arrogance, superiority, avarice, greed, corruption, recklessness, unethical practices, depersonalisation of staff members and clients, bullying, addiction to success, profits before people, and unrelenting pressures to meet unrealistic targets are just some of the behaviours that were and are still being exhibited. It was inevitable that capitalism without heart, without regard for people and which made the rich richer and the poor poorer was going to fail; a further problem was that those few mature voices that predicted the crash were aggressively ignored.

There are critical questions to be asked: how is it that we are rearing and educating males to be such poor leaders and managers? Do we seriously need to question putting men at the helm of our major political, financial, educational, health and religious organisations? Would we be better putting women into these positions of power? The answer to the latter question is that there is no guarantee that women will do any better. After all, maturity is not a gender issue, it is a human one. Furthermore, the male managers and leaders of today have been reared and educated primarily by women. Women still do the bulk of the parenting of children and primary school education is largely in the hands of female teachers (over 80 per cent primary (Irish National Teachers' Organisation, 2004) and 60 per cent secondary (Teachers' Union of Ireland, 2007)). All pre-schools are run by women. These statistics beg the question: how is it that women who have so much power in those crucial formative years of children's lives are not influencing both male and female children to become mature managers? There is no attempt here to put the responsibility for the present economic, religious, social and health service crises solely on the shoulders of women. After all, no matter what happens to us as children, as adults the matter is in our own hands and it is the responsibility of each of us to resolve any emotional baggage we are carrying from past experiences. Notoriously, males resist this essential self-exploration and have cleverly consigned such mature reflection and consequent action to the 'soft skills' bin. However, if truth be told, the responsibility for each male manager to occupy both the head and heart of their individuality is the hardest challenge for them to take on – not at all a 'soft' ride. However, it is imperative that they do because management without heart is not management at all; effective management is both a head and a heart phenomenon and not a series of mechanical tasks that many managers believe it to be.

Given that parents are the first managers and teachers are the second managers children encounter, it would appear to me that preparation and training for these key management positions need to be urgently reviewed. The experience of many children and students is the pressure to academically perform, intense competitiveness, anonymity, verbal threats, punishment of failure, over-rewarding of success and intensity around examinations and examination results. Secondary schools, in particular, are target-fixated and look to Leaving Certificate points as their main criterion for evaluating the school's effectiveness. Yet education is no index of maturity; neither is gender nor age, status nor wealth. When we view what happens in homes and classrooms, the immature behaviours that brought about the recession are not much different. What is also now clear is that the policy of education for jobs has not worked; what needs to emerge is an education for individual maturity. Is it then any wonder that the males on top turned out to be such a flop. The worrying fact is that most of our current managers and leaders continue to occupy these top positions and why oh why do we believe that they have changed their spots? A relentless examination of their attitudes and actions is called for, and I do not see the investigation into the banks carrying out such an in-depth analysis. The challenge is to find mature individuals to conduct such an investigation. The examination has to be focused on individual managers because it was not the banks or financial institutions or FÁS or the government or the Catholic Church that perpetrated neglect – *it was individuals*. I am not suggesting a witch-hunt, but I am concerned that the defensive emotional processes that ran through the veins of our top people be closely examined and that each of these individuals be supported to resolve these serious blocks to emotional, social and economic prosperity.

Leaders are Neither Born Nor Made

Leaders are neither born nor made! If it is the case that leaders are born – that it is in our genes – then 'God' has been quite deficient in the leadership stakes, as mature leadership is a rare phenomenon! In the political arena few leaders stand out – certainly, Mandela, de Klerk, Gandhi come to mind – but the reign of most leaders is brought down by their own personal problems, not by defective genes. To say that leaders are born deprives individuals of the ownership, credit and responsibility for the qualities that have brought them into a leadership role. Similarly, to say that leaders are made suggests that individuals can be moulded to be a certain way, but such conformity to the projections of others does not auger well for a mature leadership.

I believe it is more accurate to say that leaders are self-created, and to understand why some individuals become leaders and others do not, one needs to know their unique stories. Within a family, each child *creates* his own uniquely fashioned responses to the circumstances that he encounters; no two children develop the same responses. Indeed, it is true to say that each child has a different parent and a different family; in many ways each child is an only child. When any of us examines our own families it is not too difficult to see how each child within the family created his own unique repertoire of responses to the family dynamic and, subsequently, to the dynamics of school classrooms. It is the nature of these responses that determines whether or not a child will go down the road towards leadership in a particular area of endeavour – music, sport, business, art, literature, psychology, sociology, philosophy.

Leadership then isn't genetically determined, nor mystical and mysterious; it has nothing to do with having 'charisma' or other exotic behaviours (for example, the emotional exuberance of the French president, Nicolas Sarkozy).

Neither has leadership got to do with just high competence in a particular area of human expression – that is often an addiction, a way of being visible in a world where one's unique self was not affirmed.

For example, Mozart would be considered a leader among composers, but he knew nothing else other than music. By the age of seven he had done thousands of hours' practice on piano, with the shadow of an ambitious father hanging over him. However, apart from his wonderful musical compositions, Mozart was known as a 'nincompoop'. He did not at all cope with the physical, sexual, emotional, social, financial and behavioural responsibilities of everyday living. There is also the sad reality that approximately only three per cent of so-called gifted children (potential leaders!) make any important contribution to society as adults. Future leaders require a holistic approach – it is not enough to nurture a budding talent; there is the need to bed that talent in an inner self-reliance. For example, an essential attribute to effective leadership is empathy. Empathy is not simply a matter of paying attention to self and other people. It is also the capacity to identify emotional signals and make them meaningful in relationships. It would appear that many of our political leaders do not possess this emotional maturity. It is a matter to which they would do well to attend.

While there are certain responses that are characteristic of leaders – risk-taking, self-created talents, accomplishment in a particular area of endeavour – there is no guarantee that achievement will follow, let alone that the end result will be for good rather than 'evil'. Other factors enter into the development as well. For instance, leaders can be like artists, scientists and other creative thinkers (think of sport and business) who often struggle with personal vulnerabilities; as such their ability to function varies considerably even over the short run, and some potential leaders lose the struggle altogether. Leaders can often experience their creativity as restlessness, as a desire to upset other people's applecart, a compulsive need to 'do things better'. As a consequence, this kind of leader will not create a stable working or political environment; rather he or she may create a chaotic workplace or country with highly charged emotional peaks and valleys. What is often not seen is that these descriptions of leadership mirror the unresolved struggles – the peaks and valleys – of childhood, and that this hidden roller-coaster lies within the individual leader and, unless resolved, will lead to his leadership downfall. Leadership is at its most powerful when it is grounded in the context of the totality of expressions available to the unique self of a leader – physical, emotional, intellectual, behavioural, social, sexual, creative and spiritual. When such maturity is not present, people can suffer greatly from such immature leadership. Leaders have a critical responsibility to seek out opportunities to resolve their inner insecurities, and members of the social systems led by them cannot afford to collude with their hidden fears. A social system is a collective of individuals, and when the needs of a leader become *more* important than those of the collective, great neglect can occur.

Are Leaders and Managers Different?

When I wrote the book *The Mature Manager: Managing from the Inside Out*, the editor was irritated that I had not addressed the topic of leadership in the book, not to mind dedicating an entire chapter to it. I responded by saying, 'Of course not, being a manager is very different to being a leader; for me the two roles are radically different. What I would want to do is write a separate book on leadership.'

In my experience, few managers are leaders and few leaders are managers. That is not to say that the qualities for both roles cannot exist in one person, but the likelihood is low. However, there is a need for both managers and leaders in work organisations but they tend not to be comfortable bedfellows. For example, leaders sometimes respond to mundane work as to an affliction.

In one way or another, managing is one of the world's most common jobs and yet there is the disturbing fact that mediocre management is the norm. There is a further distressing reality that most people leave their jobs because of their stressful experiences with managers and that at least forty per cent of managers use a bullying style of management.

The reason for this situation is that the demands on managers are virtually impossible to meet. Managers are expected to have skills in finance, cost control, resource allocation, product development, marketing, manufacturing technology and a dozen other areas. There are also demands on managers to possess such management strategies as persuasion, negotiation, problem-solving, writing and public speaking. In many ways management is essentially a practical effort to get things done; and to fulfil his or her task, a manager needs to ensure that many people operate efficiently at different levels of status and responsibility. It does not take creativity to be a manager but it does require persistence, endurance, hard work, a concrete intelligence, analytical ability and definitely and most importantly the ability to enhance relationships with and enrol the cooperation of staff members. It would seem that we are still in the dark ages when it comes to training people how to behave like great managers. There seems to be an organisational ethos that says that managers are not responsible for people's happiness and that management is a series of mechanical responsibilities and not a set of human interactions. But the only managers who are excellent at what they do are those who manage with humanity.

Leadership is different from management, but not for the reasons some people think. Nor is leadership better than management or a replacement for it. Rather, leadership and management are two distinct and complementary systems of action. Each operates in very different ways, which are mirrors of the respective interiorities of the leaders and managers and the ways they managed to get recognition when children. Leaders aim to be different; their creativity and their being different to others fuel their leadership. Leaders may work in organisations but they never belong to them. Their self-esteem does not depend on memberships of work or social systems, work roles or social status but it does rest on their unique talent and their ability to be creative and be innovators of change. Talent is critical to continued progress in the market place and in the political field. Yet most organisations persist in perpetuating the development of managers over leaders. A hallmark of leadership is imagination; a hallmark of management is the ability to maintain order. Leaders are restless individuals, like the butterfly that goes from flower to flower, whereas managers tend to be more like busy bees that exhaust one flower before considering another. Leaders have the potential to create chaos in an organisation unless there is good and effective management present. Of course leaders are not without their insecurities and they can often feel threatened by open challenges to their ideas, as though the source of their authority, rather than their creations, was an issue. The word authority means authorship of self and when a leader confuses his sense of self with his creativity and innovations he lacks a possession of self and can become very threatened when his substitute way of getting recognition comes under what he would perceive as an attack. Such leaders need to reflect on their dependence on what lies outside them and work towards a creativity that stems from self-reliance rather than a reliance on their talent.

In considering the development of leadership and management, it is necessary to start at the earliest possible time. As seen each child in a family creates their own unique responses to the family dynamic and it can often be the case that one child goes down the road of the management of what happens in the family and the other goes the opposite direction of being the risk-taker and focusing on the development of a specific talent. The former child can be supported and directed towards being the individual who can later on guide institutions and organisations and maintain the existing balance of social relations. The latter child can be encouraged through personal mastery which will prepare him or her in their adult years to be the initiator of change and give direction in coping with change. With careful selection, nurturing, support and encouragement many people can play important management or leadership roles in work, social and political systems.

Falling Off Pedestals

Ireland has a history of putting people up on pedestals, most noteworthy priests, teachers and doctors. There is no doubt that teachers have been taken off their pedestals and the fall from grace (ironic!) of priests and other clergy is fast accelerating. The medical profession is also under pressure and the superiority and arrogance of some medical consultants is being challenged by those who seek their help and by professional colleagues.

There are two issues about being put on pedestals – one, that as an adult, you continue to accept that exalted position and, two, that those who put you there have not examined what led them to put others *above* themselves. Furthermore, it is important to realise that those who are on pedestals are not only a threat to the wellbeing of others but are also a risk to themselves. The risk to themselves is that their sense of security and recognition comes from their pedestal position and any attempt to knock them off their pedestals or any threat that emerges that will jeopardise their superior position will be met by powerful defence forces – even by the defence of covering up the sexual violation of children! Unless these individuals find their security through inhabiting their own individuality and let go of their utter dependence on awe from others, they will continue to attempt to defend their untenable position even when the evidence of their physical, sexual, intellectual, emotional or social violations is clear to others. Such apparently intractable defensiveness – sometimes, even downright denial – is located in the unconscious and will only rise to consciousness when the terror of invisibility is resolved. Intense and prolonged psychotherapy is the path to such maturity.

The process of putting individuals on pedestals is very evident in the way some parents rear their children. Parents who do everything for their children and see 'no wrong' in the children's over-demanding and extreme temper tantrums to get their own way are doing a major disservice to the children's and their own mature development. Effective parenting is about loving children for themselves and from their earliest days providing opportunities for children to take responsibility for their own needs and actions. Naturally, this process needs to be age-appropriate. Parents are not responsible *for* children; they are, however, responsible *to* their children. The responsibility *for* children militates against children taking responsibility for themselves, whereas the responsibility *to* children ensures the development of self-responsibility. Children who are spoilt – put on pedestals – have no alternative but to respond to the adoring actions of their parents; to object would mean risking rejection. Once the child's security becomes dependent on being adored and everything being done for him (for example, the Irish mother and her 'spoilt' son), it becomes terrifying for the child when there is any attempt to knock him off his pedestal. The terror is of invisibility. These children can create havoc in classrooms and communities and their parents can be at their wits' end in attempting to meet the relentless demands of these children. What the parents do not consciously realise is that they have been the authors of their own and the child's turmoil. These parents require help to examine how their own sense of invisibility led them to live their lives through their children, creating tremendous insecurity in their children, arising from the parents' own unresolved insecurities.

There is a lesson here for all of us. Whenever we find ourselves 'looking up' at another, we need to become conscious of our own inferior position – kneeling at the base of the pedestal. We need to get up off our knees, appreciate our own unique and individual person and meet others eye ('I') to eye ('I') so that each can equally support the other to be real, authentic and independent in their relationships with each other. Depending on the level of passivity present and the depth of felt unworthiness, this reclaiming of one's self worth is a long-term project. However, it is not an optional responsibility; it is an urgent and utterly critical one. Lives examined become lives lived; lives unexamined are lives not lived and an immeasurable loss to the emotional, social, spiritual and economic prosperity of a country and, ultimately, of the wider world.

The Addiction to Success

Addiction to success is very common and accounts for some of the suicides and self-harming behaviour among young people. Sadly, the emphasis on high academic and sports performance has engendered an addiction to success among both teachers and students. Parents too are success driven. It also accounts for the triple and quadruple heart bypass operations of success-driven forty-plus businessmen.

Whether it is a child, adolescent or adult who takes his or her own life because of failure to succeed, every one of us needs to sit up and ask the question: what kind of society are we creating whereby a young or older person believes they are worthless when they fail to make the high grade? I recall a mother ringing me about her daughter who was studying medicine and who had for the first time in her academic life failed an examination. The mother was distraught and told me how her daughter felt her life was over and how deeply depressed and suicidal she felt. The young woman had stopped eating and was not sleeping. She was refusing too to return to university. The mother asked, 'Can you help my daughter?' I reassured her that I could help her daughter to free herself of her addiction to success and come to a place where she could strongly assert, 'I'm not an exam result.'

The tragedy is when a parent or teacher confuses a child with their academic performance. The child intuitively knows that she can no longer attract her parents by her amazing and unique presence and that she will have to put considerable pressure on herself to gain high marks in exams in order to attract the attention of the parents. Darkness descends on her interior world and academic success becomes the substitute way of gaining some light of approval. However, the problem with the addiction to success is that you are only as good as your last success and you are terrified that the next time you may not succeed.

When a young or older person is emotionally devastated by an examination failure, a much more serious examination is required of what has brought the person to such a dependent place and such a confusion of self with success. When the parents of the young person are equally devastated, then an examination of the ethos of the family is necessary. The latter involves examining the nature of the relationship each parent has with self and the quality of the relationship each parent has with the child who is trauma-tised. It is frequently the case that a parent's addiction to success is more seriously and deeply rooted than that of their son or daughter. In the case of the medical student mentioned above, her mother asked me several times, 'How soon will you have my daughter back to university?' A mother who loves her daughter for her true self would have asked the question, 'How soon can you return my daughter to a place of wellbeing?' It is a reality that we spill the beans on our insecurities and vulnerabilities any time we open our mouths!

The person who is addicted to success is greatly impeded from getting on with her life. Indeed the greatest impediment to progress is success. The student who is mature and operates from an inner stronghold of self may well be disappointed with a particular test result, but she won't be devastated. On the contrary, while acknowl-edging her disappointment, she will embrace the disappointing result as an opportunity to learn and from which to progress. The difference between the person who loves to learn and the person who is success driven is that the former views learning as an adventure, while the latter sees it as a strain, a worry, a pressure. The person who is addicted will also be highly competitive, whereas the person who loves learning will be competitive with self, which is the healthiest form of competition.

Success addiction does not add to the security, development, productivity and creativity of a society. On the contrary, it takes a huge toll on the wellbeing of the individual herself and on all others who live, study and work with this overdrive. Leaders have a major responsibility to restore a love of learning to classrooms, a love of work to workplaces and, mostly, a love of person to families and schools.

Addiction To What Others Think

A common addiction is the addiction to what others think and say about you. Answering the questions set out below will provide some index of the extent of your craving for approval or acknowledgement.

- Do you ever find yourself asking for approval with questions like 'Did I do a good job?' 'How do I look?' (and then find yourself disappointed by the reply)?
- Do you have difficulty in saying 'no' to other people's requests of you?
- Do you ever demand affection from others which you then don't receive and as a result feel hurt and let down?
- Do you ever feel inwardly resentful when somebody fails to acknowledge a kindness or favour you have done for them?
- Do you have a 'need to be needed' or a 'need to be liked'?
- Do you conform to the wishes of others without consideration of your own wishes and likes?
- Do you ever feel 'everything is my fault' and then spend time feeling guilty?
- Do you worry about what others think of you following meeting them?

Answering 'yes' to any one of these questions indicates your actions may sometimes be triggered by a deep-seated desire for approval. This need for approval relates to childhood when we cleverly tried to find ways to please the significant people in our lives, those on whom we depended for our very survival. This drive for approval arises in a family or classroom or other significant setting where there is constant disapproval, or lack of encouragement, affection, belief in or warmth.

It is important to view an addiction, whether to a particular way of behaving or to a substance, as a *substitute* for the real thing. It is devastating for children when their natural ways of gaining recognition do not work – their smile, their raising their arms up to be picked up, their humour, their tenderness, excitement, eagerness, responsiveness to being nurtured, their expressiveness, spontaneity, adventurous behaviour, difference and individuality. The emergence of an addiction means that conformity to an important person's ways is being demanded and woe betide the child who does not dutifully respond. For example, a parent or teacher who is dominant and believes she is always right will demand and command acquiescence to her beliefs and ways of behaving. The child who wisely conforms ingeniously develops the addiction to what this adult says because he knows the dangers of harsh abandonment should he not conform. The wisdom in being addicted to what others think is to try and anticipate what they want of you so that you can offset rejection and the overwhelming hurt and darkness that accompany it. It is essential for children's survival of over-controlling and demanding parents, teachers and other significant adults in their lives that they find a strategy, a substitute way of gaining approval. Pleasing them and worrying and watching out for what these adults think, say and do is one powerful way. However, there is no substitute for the real thing. Children and adults who continue to be addicted to what others think are in constant fear of not identifying what are the demands of the adults they fear most. There is no security, no peace, no relief, no contentment, and no real love – just a way of trying to offset rejection and hurt.

Whatever our upbringing has been, as adults we cannot change how we were reared, but we can change how we relate to ourselves, and, indeed, to others and especially children. While children, out of dependence, necessarily develop an addiction to what others think and say, adults need no longer depend on others for their survival. This need to separate out from dependence on significant adults in one's life is crucial to becoming one's own person and living one's own life and no longer the life of a significant other. We no longer need to waste our precious energy and creativity seeking external approval, which, inevitably, leads us to act in ways which do not serve our progress in living. We need to find the support to develop the ability to value and approve of ourselves and to stand on our own two capable feet. Rather than defensively giving our power away and becoming victim to others by blaming them for whatever is missing from our lives, we can enjoy creating it ourselves. We need to reclaim our right to live our own unique and individual lives. Where the addiction is deep-seated, considerable support and sometimes professional psychotherapeutic help may be needed for us to cut the ties that have bound us. Persist in the seeking of that support so that a full recovery of one's true self is attained.

Dangerous To Be Male

Dire statistics demonstrate that being a male is far more dangerous than being a female. Men die on average five to seven years earlier than women; a high percentage of men die quite soon after retiring from work; ninety per cent of violence is perpetrated by males; most road deaths are caused by male drivers; one in four women is subjected to violence by men. The gender ratio of completed suicide is three to one in favour of males. Men are notorious for not going to a medical doctor with enduring physical symptoms. Some thirty per cent of fathers disappear from their children's lives within one year of marital separation. Unmarried or separated/divorced men, who do not find another partner, have a lower life expectancy than women who find themselves living alone. Men's psycho-social wellbeing is particularly affected by their not having an emotional vocabulary. Alcohol and drug addictions are far more prevalent among males and the source of these addictions is often the bottling up of feelings and the fear of being laughed at or appearing 'weak' should they express emergency feelings.

On the education side, girls are outdoing boys across all the academic subjects, an average differential of nine per cent in favour of the girls. Studies are consistently showing that girls are more educationally motivated, work harder and attain higher class results than boys in co-educational schools. One of the common explanations given is that boys are wired differently to girls and hence the difference in educational achievement. I find this explanation astoundingly arrogant and question, 'How come, when over all the years boys were outdoing girls across most subjects, particularly higher mathematics, physics and science, the suggestion was not made that boys were wired differently to girls?' It is far more likely that the reason for the difference in academic achievement between the sexes is that girls are more motivated and do work harder. After all, they were the oppressed gender – and still are to a large degree – except that now they have found a way to liberate themselves through education. Boys may still be sitting on the laurels of a patriarchal society and, rather than being condemned to 'biological inferiority', it would be better if belief were shown in them and encouragement given to them to more seriously take on the challenges of education. This notion of a biologically defective gender is particularly prevalent in the epidemic labelling of boys (three to one ratio in favour of boys) with ADD, ADHD, and ODD (oppositional defiance disorder). How is it that modern women are giving birth to so many biologically deficient boys, resulting in these syndromes? Or is there another more logical and verifiable possibility – boys are reared differently to girls. One female professional friend asked me why do boys turn out the way they do: 'After all, we their mothers cuddle them, love them, dote on them.' I replied, 'The reason some boys turn out the way they do is because mothers don't ask for anything in return.' It is for this reason so many women complain of men being 'takers', but women forget that these men's mothers did not provide the opportunities on a daily basis for boys to engage in the multiplicity of ways of giving as well as receiving. Good relationships are about give and take and it is essential that boys and girls experience and are realistically expected to take and give in family relationships. Rearing and educating boys is not about 'boys being boys'; it is about 'boys being human' and being given the opportunities to experience the full breadth of human qualities, both head and heart. It is gross neglect not to have boys involved in the nurturing, emotional, expressive, comforting, supporting, listening, sharing and domestic responsibilities that are part and parcel of family life. There needs to be a definite balance between outward activities (which have been over-emphasised) and inward activities (which have been hugely under-emphasised). What needs to be true for boys needs also to be true for girls. Girls, too, need to be reared to be fully human.

I am quite convinced that what lies at the core of men's problems in living is how they are parented and how they are taught. A serious reflection is required by heads of families, schools and relevant government departments to look at these fundamental issues that deeply influence and underpin why it is more dangerous to be male than female.

MALEs Ireland

MALEs (Men as Learners and Elders) Ireland is a new organisation set up in 2004 as a 'school for male spiritual development'. This organisation is to be welcomed alongside an increasing number of groups and programmes to support men experiencing psychological, social and spiritual difficulties. My one reservation about such groups is that they might contribute to the long-term polarisation of males and females that has not been a healthy phenomenon in Irish culture. Nonetheless, these groups are a starting place, particularly because many men are frequently put off self-help groups because these are usually dominated by women, whose way of relating can be challenging to those men who are emotionally inhibited. My recommendation is that men, when ready, join a heterogeneous group; after all, mixed-gender schools are healthier places for young people's overall development.

There is no doubt that men need all the help they can get. There is a widely observed crisis in Irish men which has manifested itself most profoundly in the alarmingly high rate of suicide and road accidents, particularly among young men. Other indicators are addiction to work, violence, high rates of workplace bullying, alcohol and drug addictions. The high rate of marital breakdown is yet another barometer of males (and females) in crisis.

Certainly, male groups need to address how men view themselves (self-esteem), how men are in relationships (emotional and social literacy), how men see themselves as fathers, the meaning of work in their lives, what meaning does existence and the world hold for them (philosophy of life) and whether or not there is a spiritual dimension to existence. On male spiritual development, the way the organisation *MALEs* describes its spiritual aims appears quite similar to psychotherapy. Certainly, the dividing line between psychological and spiritual meaning appears confused, even though a speaker for the organisation insisted that the two paths are quite distinct. The organisation was at pains to point out that its workshops are not a substitute for therapy. However, the spokesperson's description of psychotherapy was highly inaccurate when he said that 'traditional therapy generally helps to build a healthy ego so that a person can engage in society and relationships. It may not necessarily fulfil them, but at the end of the day it gives them a certain ground on which to stand to be able to deal with life.' Contrary to the latter description, psychotherapy is about helping individuals to free themselves of their ego by helping them to realise their own true self. Ego is the defensive shadow world that a person creates and hides behind to reduce the possibilities of hurt, humiliation and rejection. This defensive process starts in childhood and, unless reflected upon, strengthens and deepens as individuals grow older. In psychotherapy there is no such thing as 'a healthy ego'. Establishing a strong and solid sense of self from which nobody can demean, exile, exclude or lessen your presence is the aim of dynamic psychotherapy. Certainly, I believe that coming to a place of possession of one's authentic self is the launch pad for exploring a spiritual path, but it is not to be confused with it.

Individuals can feel psychologically and socially confident, but may lack spiritual confidence or have no spiritual beliefs. It seems to me that, having realised a true sense of one's own unique self, there may then arise a need for a deeper sense of meaning, a deeper sense of connection with the universe, a deep need to acknowledge that there may be something bigger than the self, whatever that may be. Human search for meaning beyond one's own personal existence is as old as humankind, and scientific developments have not dampened such a quest. It may well be that spirituality workshops will cross the line into psychological territory (this can be a two-way street), but this is in keeping with the thoughts of some of the great spiritual leaders. For example, Christ clearly taught that the love of self (psychotherapy) is the foundation for the love of others (sociology) and that both of these loves can transcend to a love of God (spirituality). A thousand years before Christ, Buddha, the great teacher of spiritual enlightenment, said that 'you can travel the entire world and not find anybody more deserving of love than yourself'.

Gender Inequalities

Statistics on gender differences in Ireland across a number of key social issues may have left women wondering what exactly they have to do to gain equality with men. The statistics showed that women, though more educated, earn 14.7 per cent less on average than a man doing the same job (2002, Department of Enterprise, Trade and Employment); women also do most of the housework and childcare and also are far more likely to wind up looking after the elderly and infirm. The two apparent advantages are that they live six to eight years longer (2009, World Health Organisation) – although they end up poorer than men – and are unlikely to wind up in prison. What requires major reflection is the appalling statistic that over ninety per cent of prisoners in Ireland are male (2001, Irish Prison Service Report).

Certainly, the fact that women receive a much lower salary than men doing the same job is a serious social injustice and requires immediate action. It would appear that women need to create their own unions to campaign for equal and fair payment.

On the face of it, the statistic that women are still doing over seventy per cent of housework and childcare (2005, Equality Authority and the Economic and Social Research Institute) appears grossly unfair and I certainly would be advocating a 50/50 situation where there are two-parent families. However, another way of looking at the statistic is that most men are missing out on the pleasurable and fulfilling aspects of child-rearing and, indeed, home-making, and one wonders what are men doing about this intolerable situation? The statistics showed that more and more women are working outside the home but continue to carry the major responsibility within the home. For this reason married women with children have become the most-at-health-risk group in Irish society.

The questions have to be asked: why do men continue to occupy ninety per cent of the top financial and political positions, are more likely to be seen as 'non-nourishing' beings and are far more likely to perpetrate violence? At least women can appreciate that they are less 'status driven' than men, are generally appreciated as 'nourishing beings' and are far less likely to resort to violence as a means of resolving conflict. Long may these qualities continue and become balanced with mature ambition, ability to receive nourishment, and assertiveness. There is no doubt that women have made significant moves along these particular dimensions of human qualities but, as the statistics show, a lot more needs to be done. I have no doubt that this will continue and will begin to change how women rear their female and male children. Typically, male children are steered away from the qualities that women are most noted for – nurturance, kindness, tenderness, empathy, listening, compassion – and steered towards the qualities that men are most noted for – aggression, drive, taking control, ambition, invention. The reverse tends to happen for female children.

Even though women are still visibly disadvantaged in the areas mentioned, it is important that sight is not lost of the fact that, albeit in a different way, men are also disadvantaged. There are the beginnings of a male movement seeking equality with women in the parenting of children and gaining recognition from care professionals and the courts for their right and ability to nurture children. An equally pressing quest is to resolve the strong male propensity to aggression and violence as means of resolving conflict. The future of society always lies with adults, and unless men reflect on how their aggressive behaviour poses such a threat to the well-being of others and, indeed, themselves, little progress will occur. Children have to survive the defensive behaviours of adults, and many children learn to 'fight fire with fire' or to displace their rage around being lessened and demeaned onto others. Other children resort to passivity and 'fight shy' of those adults, mostly male, who are likely to physically or verbally violate their presence. Those children (or adults) who unconsciously engage passivity and withdrawal as their defences often become the targets of those children (or adults) who employ bullying as their defensive weapon. Empowering those who bully and who are passive is fundamental to the resolution of aggression and violence in society.

Each male and female requires the opportunities to express the full breadth of human qualities and for each to realise his or her giftedness and potential. The earlier in life these opportunities are provided, the better for each individual, male or female, and for society as a whole.

What Lies Behind the Mars–Venus Myth

A new book by a feisty Oxford professor of language and communication, Deborah Cameron, is determined to lay to rest the simplistic idea that when it comes to communication, men and women are essentially different. Her book has the long-winded title (which in some ways shoots her theory in the foot), *The Myth of Mars and Venus: Do Men and Women Really Speak Different Languages?* However, she quickly puts this slip to rights with a few well-aimed statistics. She shows convincingly that the difference in language use between men and women is statistically negligible. Women don't interrupt more than men nor are they more talkative or empathic in conversation; nor are they less assertive or poorer at verbal reasoning. To drive her point home that men and women are pretty similar when it comes to communication, she cites the wildly unsubstantiated claim in a popular science book, *The Female Brain*, that women utter 20,000 words a day while men manage only 7,000. Subsequent reprints of the book quietly deleted the invented figures. Incidentally, statistics mask the fact that some individual men and women do have profound fears of speaking openly about their inner and outer lives.

Following her successful demolition of the myth that men are from Mars and women are from Venus and her demonstration that both men and women are from Earth, Deborah Cameron poses an important question: why is the Mars–Venus myth so popular today, particularly among educated Western women? She appears puzzled by this conundrum because it would appear that the women in contemporary Western society have nothing to gain from stereotypes about male–female behaviour. Contrary to her well-argued defence of the similarities between men and women, she surprisingly concludes that when it comes to communication, both men and women 'haven't a clue'. She misses here the unerring intelligence of human behaviour and, in particular, the employment by women of the powerful weapon of mythical male–female differences in the battle between the sexes. While I totally agree with the reality of there being no differences in how men and women as distinct groups communicate, this does not hold true for the power position of men and women. In society, the inequality of power between men and women is very evident in religion, politics, high finance, leadership and management positions, sexuality and parenting. Certainly, the gap is closing in some of these arenas, but it remains a challenging position for women to play a far larger role in politics, religion and high finance. Until there is equality of power between the sexes, both men and women will attempt to intelligently exploit the mythical gender differences and the sexual stereotypes that keep men and women polarised.

What would have reinforced Deborah Cameron's arguments would have been to define the nature of communication. The present difficulties in communication, not just between men and women but also between men and men and women and women, arose from past relationships where it became unsafe for the individuals to practise genuine, authentic, direct and clear communication. Communication arises spontaneously from our interiority, and when this is dark and insecure, communication will automatically reflect that inner turmoil. Likewise, when individuals have a solid interiority, their communication will automatically be open, sincere, direct and clear, except, of course, in situations of high threats to their wellbeing. It is when the nature of the relationship within individuals changes that relationships between people change. In other words, it is maturity that determines effective communication. Age, gender, status, power, education are no indices of maturity, but love of and responsibility for self and all our actions are. Each of us, both men and women, need to come down to earth and find union with self so that communication with others promotes union between people. This is a mighty challenge in a world where there exists great threats to being oneself and it is in this great struggle to become independent that both men and women are, in no uncertain terms, earthlings.

A Matter of Time

A friend recently requested an article on time. What prompted her request was her frequent experience of hearing the phrase 'I'm so busy I haven't time . . .' She correctly pointed out that it is one's response to this statement that counts. After all, what the other person says is about him or her; equally, your response to what another person says is about you. An examination of that response is what is required. Her reaction to 'I'm so busy I haven't time . . .' is that she feels 'almost redundant'. This response would appear to be self-esteem related as if 'being busy' means 'I am of worth'. The possibility arises here of an addiction to work. This comes from the childhood experiences of conditional relating manifested in such expectations 'Be good', 'Be perfect', 'Be hard working', 'Be clever' and 'Don't be a waster'.

The phrase 'I'm so busy I haven't time' begs the question, 'Haven't time for what?' Very often it can be the situation where 'being busy' involves not having time for partner, one's own children, friends, family of origin, basic human kindness and most of all for self. It is only in finding time for self that you are in a place to find time to be with another. Furthermore, it is in the experiencing of no-thing-ness (no doing) that we realise our fullness and the fullness of another.

There is nothing more devastating for a child than when she discovers that one or both of her parents have 'no time for her', meaning that there is an absence of affection, warmth and celebration of the child's unique presence. It is often the case that a parent who has 'no time' for a child pays little attention to 'self' (time for self). I have worked with many young people who complain and are bitterly hurt that their father or mother had no time for them. It is frequently the case that as young adults these children point blank refuse to work! In these cases it is often the situation that the father was addicted to work or alcohol or sports. These addictions are substitute actions that have the function of 'filling the void within' and, sadly, means that the father is not in a welfare place to meet the love needs of his children and, indeed, his life partner. A sad statistic is that approximately thirty per cent of fathers disappear from their children's lives following separation from their wives. For the other seventy per cent of separated fathers, it is sometimes the case that 'promises' to their children are not followed through and mothers are left to 'pick up the pieces' of the overwhelming hurt and disappointment the children suffer. Having 'time for our loved ones' arises from 'having time for ourselves' – a challenge that exists for many of us as adults.

The second question my friend put to me was 'Is time age-related?' It certainly appears that our attitude to time is largely determined by what stage of life we are at. We can all recall when we were children having very little concept of time and irritatingly asking 'Are we there yet?' Teenagers often complain of being bored and that a day feels like an eternity for them. Adults in their twenties, thirties and forties tend to live their lives as if they are going to live forever! In contrast, the phrases that tend to be present on the lips of the over-sixties are 'Where has time gone?' and 'Time and tide waits for no man' (or woman) and 'Little time left'. This is sensible thinking because it gets us, maybe for the first time, to treasure each moment and use it creatively and productively to enrich our inner and outer lives. It is interesting too that spirituality is far more prevalent among the over-sixties than those in early and mid-adulthood. Does this need for spiritual meaning arise from fear of death (and the search for meaning is to allay that fear) or does it arise from our inner nature, which may be timeless? A wonderful writer, Stephen Levine, author of *Who Dies?*, *A Year to Live* and other books, says that 'The reason why human beings are preoccupied with immortality is because they are immortal.'

3 It's Not the System, It's the Individual

Are We Victims or Creators?

Sigmund Freud believed that human beings experienced three tremendous blows to their sense of importance in the universe when it was discovered:

> one, that we as a species descended from animals,
> two, that the earth is not the centre of the universe, and
> three, that we are victims of unconscious forces.

From my own point of view, evolution does not diminish the dignity and the incredible nature of human beings. As regards the earth not being the centre of the universe, it is part of an increasingly expanding and mysterious universe and, as humans, we possess the limitless power to view, understand and harness the stupendous resources of the universe.

It is with Freud's third blow – where he believes people are victims of unconscious forces – that I take particular issue. Freud believed that only he, a psychoanalyst, could unravel the workings of the unconscious but that individuals themselves were at the mercy of these unconscious forces. His notion of 'Freudian slips' – more colloquially known as 'slips of the tongue' – further reinforced his belief that people had no control over what arises from the unconscious.

Freud was not the only one to perceive humans as victims. The theory that strongly reacted to Freud's focus on the past and the unconscious was conditioning theory. Pavlov and Skinner both believed we are victims of our conditioning and that the intervention required is one of de-conditioning and re-conditioning here and now in the present. Cognitive theories further the behavioural conditioning model by suggesting we are victims of our thought processes. Therapies such as Beck's Cognitive Theory, Ellis's Rational Emotive Behaviour Therapy (REBT) and Neuro-Linguistic Programming (NLP) set out to identify the 'negative thinking and talking patterns' you have become victim of and how you can be deprogrammed and programmed to think and talk in positive and optimistic ways. Many religions had a deterministic view of the fate of human beings, even believing that we can be possessed by 'evil' spirits. There are also theories that believe that our behaviour is determined by genes or biological or chemical imbalances. The latter medical model understanding of human behaviour led to the revolving door in psychiatry and the fostering of hopelessness.

The drawback to seeing individuals as victims is that they are given no credit for the thoughts, dreams, Freudian slips or actions they manifest. Neither is any meaning given to these experiences. There is an additional issue – if we are victims, how can real and mature change ever be brought about? Are we then to become victims of psychoanalysts, geneticists, biologists, behavioural and cognitive therapists and neuro-linguistic programmers? An interesting question to ask is: do these therapists see themselves as victims?

What if the situation is the reverse of what these theories say; what if we are creators of our thoughts, dreams, feelings, actions and Freudian slips? What if the human being assesses very astutely the physical, sexual, emotional, intellectual, behavioural and social dangers to his or her presence (and authentic self-expressions) in the particular social system in which those threats arise – family, school, community, church, workplace? What if in determining the threats the person either unconsciously or consciously develops their own particular ways of reducing the threats to their wellbeing and at the same time find a substitute means of holding wholeness? And what if the person who is in a place of the inner stronghold of self-realisation and self-possession challenges the threatening responses of others – where does such independence, compassion and authenticity come from? Furthermore, if, indeed, individuals are creators, it means that they can be supported to understand and take responsibility for their own responses – when the safety from within or without to do so is present.

Take the situation when a baby encounters harsh rejection from her mother; the baby wisely finds a way to reduce the frightening impact of the mother's behaviour by totally avoiding eye contact with her and avoiding reaching out to be picked up. Such an avoidance creation means the child has found a way to offset the darkness of abandonment and hold onto her sense of wholeness – albeit in a substitute way. It would be unwise of the child – even later on when she has developed language – to voice the truth of the situation, unless the mother has resolved the creative intentions of her not warming to the child. A possibility that might explain the mother's behaviour is that any attempt by her to embrace the child may propel her back to her own abandonment experiences when she was a child.

That we are creators of our own responses is very much borne out by the reality that each child within a family responds – or fashions their own responses – to each of their parent's responses to them. How many times do we hear, 'each of my children is so different?' It is now believed that each child has a different parent, that each student has a different teacher and that each employee has a different manager. The parent, teacher or manager that attempts to treat all his charges in the same way is creatively manifesting fear of expressing his own individuality. Whether we like it or not, as children and adults, every time we move, talk, take action, or withdraw, we spill the beans on our interiority. Such a spilling of the beans is creatively designed in the hope that some mature adult out there will spot the need for safety and support that the person's substitute behaviours are crying out for. Too often, it is the case that such symptoms are flown in vain.

It's Not the System, It's the Person

One of the very powerful ways that individuals distance themselves from responsibility to their actions is to blame the system – the family, the organisation, the government, the school, the workplace, the church, society. There are those who believe that a social system has intelligence apart from the intelligence of the individual members of the system. My question is: 'where is this system's intelligence located?' I can locate the intelligence of a person in their brain. It appears to me that it is remarkably clever of an individual, who possesses undoubted limitless intelligence, to abrogate responsibility for self and for his or her actions by blaming the system. I have encountered such a response so often: 'sure that's the way society is.' My reply is: define society. Surely, any social system is a collective of individuals and it is the level of maturity that each person brings to the system that determines the system's ethos. Sometimes it takes only one individual – who comes with considerable maturity – to change a system so that the wellbeing of each member of the system becomes the primary aim of the collective. Equally, sometimes it takes only one person who comes with deep inner turmoil to darken the ethos of a system, particularly when that person is at the system's helm.

When a politician hides their actions, values and beliefs behind 'government policy' they cease to take responsibility for their actions and the maturity of their leadership needs to be seriously challenged. This happened in the 2010 besieged Irish government, but what proved to be of even greater concern is that those members of the government party that did not back the government's budget policy on medical cards for the over seventies were dropped from their positions. It would appear that the expression of one's own values and beliefs was not supported by the leader of the last government! The wise thing to do would have been to promote the individuals who had the courage to question the leader's judgement. It is not a sign of mature leadership to threaten loss of status for being authentic. It induces fear and a profound unsafety for genuine and open expression of difference. No doubt, the argument will be that the 'government needs the loyalty of its front and back benchers', but it is the mature leader who recognises that an individual's first loyalty needs to be to what he or she perceives as what is true for him or her. Given that much of the present financial crisis has resulted from those individuals with most power in the banks depersonalising customers and employees and turning a blind ethical eye to what would have been best for the collective of individuals – the country – the similar behaviour of the then government leader was a great source of concern. Nonetheless, each of us who voted in that government and each of us who colluded with the depersonalisation policies and lack of transparency of the banks need to examine and take responsibility for our own responses. It is not governments that neglect their people – it is people in government that do it. It is not work organisations that bully employees, but individuals who bully colleagues. It is not the family that is dysfunctional; it is individual members of the family that perpetrate neglect. It is not guns that kill people; it is people who kill people. It is not drugs that harm people; it is people taking drugs that cause harm.

In the kindest possible way, each of us needs to be challenged firmly when we project responsibility for our actions onto the system or another person or substance. No progress can be made in bettering the lives of the collective of individuals without individuals taking responsibility for self and their own actions. This is particularly expedient for those in positions of power – parents, teachers, heads of financial, health and other work organisations, bishops, priests and, most of all, political leaders. Those who hide behind the defence 'it's the system' are being very clever in offsetting being criticised for their actions; but it is the mature leader who can admit to mistakes and failures and progress from learning from unwise decisions.

I believe then that it is the individual who lies at the heart of each social system. I further believe that the more each individual takes responsibility for self and their actions, the more mature society will be.

Banking on the Banks to be Mature

I frequently refer to Gandhi's seven deadly sins in society: pleas ure without conscience, knowledge without character, wealth without work, science without humanity, politics without principle, commerce without humanity and worship without sacrifice.

The 'sin' or, more aptly, the 'omission' that commerce without humanity describes is what has brought about the present major crisis in the banking world. The serious omission of consideration for people in their financial practices sounded the death knell for the banking world a long time ago, and the rise of greed – making 'the few' obscenely rich and the pressure to keep increasing profits – further darkened the corporate world of banking. This fixation on profits and relentless profit-making led to a depersonalisation, not only of the banks' customers, but also of their employees. The bank's clientele's age, state of health or personal circumstances did not matter. What mattered was making money.

Leaders and managers of organisations – financial, social, political and educational – that lose sight of people and put the goals of the organisation before the wellbeing of people – employees and customers alike – inevitably implode. This present implosion in the banking world has been absolutely necessary – like an earthquake that occurs to restore ecological equilibrium – to wake up the corporate world of banking to its inhumane practices that largely were left go unchallenged. Indeed, not only did the customers not protest, but governments placed too much trust in banks. For the various governments that are presently 'bailing out' the banks, the hope is that these governments will insist that banks urgently and seriously review their values and their practices and restore humaneness to their financial dealings. This social accountability needs to be a *sine qua non* of financial institutions and will require close monitoring for the foreseeable future. It is going to take people a long time to trust the banks – especially since their promises of 'trust us' have been so hugely betrayed. Trust can only be built up through visible and transparent actions, not through 'empty' words – that the heart is returning to banks' servicing of their customers, mortgage holders and shareholders. A massive emotional debt, too, is owed to the banks' employees who have been treated as resources, dare not rock the boat or have a life outside the system. The banks are not alone in the depersonalising of employees, but wherever such neglect occurs it needs to be strongly challenged.

The corporate world needs to be convinced that contented, non-stressed employees are much more likely to sustain an organisation's progress and profitability. Equally, customers who feel they are personalised will maintain a loyalty to their bank. For many years I have argued with banks' personnel that the depersonalisation of their customers (and staff) and the provision of a faceless centralised service would prove counterproductive. Little did I know how prophetic those beliefs were to be.

The present major crisis in the financial sector provides an incredible opportunity for the corporate banking world to examine its values and practices. It is important that customers, employees and governments do not allow the heads of banks to slide out of that critical responsibility. Effective leaders and effective managers operate from both a head and heart place. The governors of banks lost their heart and, without it, lost their head as well and, as a result, we have all suffered. Will they learn from it? The opportunity is there, but the emotional and social safety to learn is essential to the emergence of maturity and balance in banking practices.

In light of the foregoing, I believe that what I call the 'seven deadly omissions' in work organisations require serious exploration:

- organisations without humanity
- leadership without maturity
- management without relationship
- work without dignity
- ethos without enlightened ethical practices
- profits without compassion
- success without separateness.

One of my own aims is to transform the human resources approach (which has lost sight of people) in organisations to a human relationships one and to demonstrate how this makes for progress in achieving the goals of work organisations. I believe what also needs to be closely examined is what makes for mature leadership and management and the training and selection requirements for these critical processes. Most of all, I would wish to empower employees to make sure that the work they do and the workplace is worthy of their dignity. When it is not, then serious questions need to be asked and mature actions taken.

The Seven Deadly 'Sins' of Work Organisations

Further to the foregoing article, I wish to write on two of the sins of omission mentioned: work organisations without humanity and leadership without maturity. In many ways, these two omissions are inter-related. A work organisation is a collective of individuals who are operating within the work system: those on the inside are part of the system; those on the outside are not part of the system. An organisation is said to be *functional* when it is fulfilling its goals and *dysfunctional* when it is not. However, there is a flaw in that logic, because the goals of the organisation may not be inclusive of the wellbeing of some of the members of the organisation. A common complaint of employees is of anonymity. It is often the case that it is the 'few' at the top of the hierarchy of power within the organisation that determine the values and goals of the organisation. When those leaders operate from an authoritarian, superior and supremely immature place, the goals of the organisation will reflect such immaturity. The telling question is: who determines the maturity of leaders? After all, education, status, achievements, wealth, age and success are no indices of maturity. Indeed, the contrary can be the case. Maturity is marked by the possession of the qualities of self-reliance, equality with others, independence, a work ethic that arises from a place of love for self and others, fairness, justice, consideration for others and a recognition that employees have a life inside themselves and outside the organisation, an ability to individualise employees, possession of a value of not putting profits before people and not confusing self with success. Furthermore, mature leaders operate from both a heart *and* head place. Notoriously, many leaders, especially male, operate purely from the head and the absence of the balancing power of the heart can mean a ruthless and heartless leadership. Such a leadership, inevitably, will lead to organisational conflict, even the collapse of the organisation. It strikes me as hugely neglectful when leaders of organisations, who from a place of profound immaturity are permitted to use their power to overpower or dis-empower employees, are never required to examine their level of emotional and social maturity. A life unexamined can lead to untold neglect and hurt of others. From an organisational point of view, a leader whose life goes unexamined can result in considerable organisational dysfunction. Policies, values and structures need to be in place so that the individual leader does not become more powerful than the organisation. Other people within the organisation need to be able to have recourse to structures and procedures that strongly challenge the immature actions of leaders. Too often, in the political arena we have seen that the absence of such 'protectors' of the political system can have disastrous results on a country's people. We can point to Mugabe in Zimbabwe, but we have had our own leaders who have not examined their lives! The enmeshment between leaders and the work organisation is a phenomenon that sorely needs to be challenged – for all concerned, including the leaders. The critical question is which members of the organisation are going to do that, because an organisation in itself has no intelligence to change anything – only the people within the organisation can effect change.

Work organisations that are functional ensure that the wellbeing of each person within the organisation matters and counts before profits and success. The organisation certainly does not lose sight of its goals, but it knows that 'people first' is the life-blood of a progressive and enduring work organisation. The provision of opportunities for employees to further develop their potential is also a priority. A mature organisation is also conscious of the influence of wider systems outside the work organisation – particularly the family and the community. Such an organisation is both family and community friendly and promotes a healthy relationship with these other social systems.

When work organisations are dysfunctional, the mass of employees need to employ their power to challenge the untenable situation. This did not happen in the banks and I know it is not occurring within many multinational companies. However, it is good for employees to recognise that without their cooperation, organisations cease to function. In offering mature cooperation, employees are saving themselves and the organisation.

The Business of Education

There is an emerging debate about the involvement of business in education. Governments spend huge sums of money on education and because it is a stated aim of the EU to invest even more in education, government spending will need to increase. On the face of it, allowing funds from the business world appears a sound idea, but 'there is no such thing as a free business lunch!' What strings would be attached is an important consideration. The stated educational objectives of the business world would be to create a talented, creative, highly articulate and knowledgeable workforce. Businesses require students who are highly achieving, who can invent new products and who can speak several languages. Such a graduate workforce, it is postulated, would maintain Europe's competitive edge. At the present time, schools are producing too many students whose achievements are mediocre. There is an acute shortage of scientists, engineers, mathematicians, researchers and decision-makers. The business world believes schools are teaching the wrong subjects and that teachers fail to see the bigger picture.

Business-funded schools would aim to correct the situation regarding subjects taught and would bring business acumen to the running of such schools. Those who support the involvement of the business community believe it has the money that schools and universities require and that it possesses the right experience and expertise in motivating people.

While I agree in principle with the contribution that businesses *could* make to education, I would question whether business personnel are in any way more mature than the teachers of whom they are critical. After all, anonymity is one of the major complaints of employees in the workplace and up to forty per cent of managers employ a bullying style of management. Absenteeism is high, as are stress-related illnesses and retirement on ill-health grounds. It appears also that financial prosperity does not equal emotional prosperity and that chief executive officers in the business world are not necessarily emotionally mature. Indeed, it is known that many of them are work-addicted or success-addicted and that marital and family difficulties or breakdown are common. Many of these 'high-achievers' suffer heart attacks in their early forties.

My other concern is that business-funded schools will be motivated by profit and not by people and I'm sure in return for their money they will want to cherry-pick the schools with the best prospects, to determine the school subjects and to attract the best teachers, who will be regularly performance assessed. The involvement too of the private sector raises issues of democratic accountability, since many of the current contracts, for example in Germany and Britain, are lengthy and span electoral cycles, making it difficult to hold either the company or the government to account.

One other worry is the present reality of considerable amounts of money being spent on so-called 'gifted' children. Only three per cent of these children make any important social and economic contribution as adults. The reason for this is the confusion of knowledge with intelligence and the 'hot-housing' of a particular branch of knowledge – mathematics, music, physics – which misses out on the holistic development of these children, who do not tend to cope with the multiplicity of emotional, social, sexual, educational, intellectual and occupational demands in their late teens and early adulthood. My feeling is that the business world can be blinkered when it comes to the pursuit of their goals and I'm not convinced that they are necessarily the best people to become leaders in education.

All of the foregoing points to a fundamental difference in philosophy between educationalists and business people. It appears to me that the business world confuses training with education, and teachers who view education as being primarily about the personal development of each student are resisting the utilitarian approach of the business world. We are all aware of employees who feel that the organisation they work for owns them lock, stock and barrel. My fear is that the business-run schools and colleges will view students only as potential resources rather than people.

A matter to which business people need to give serious consideration is that the possession of skills does not guarantee efficiency, creativity, productivity and effectiveness. Maturity is an essential requirement for work effectiveness, and leaders' and managers' attendance to their own and students' and employees' social, sexual, physical and spiritual development is critical to this mature process.

What schools and colleges need are people whose vision is broad-minded and who recognise that the emotional and social development of students is just as important as the development of a knowledge of mathematics, science, physics and chemistry.

Beyond the Usual Politics

The age-old dictum of Socrates, 'Know Yourself', is as relevant today as it was two and half thousand years ago; it is especially relevant to our politicians. Leadership positions are privileged positions accorded to individuals for a time by the electorate (us, the people). Such positions are always accompanied by sacred responsibilities towards the people. They need to be taken up as such. This is a practice that demands persistent effort and not mere lip service. However, such responsible action on the part of our politicians is only possible when they know themselves. The more common experience is that politicians, even the best of them, are often impelled to put their spin on whatever they think the electorate should be thinking rather than inviting us to make up our own minds, and being more open and honest about their biases and 'dirty tricks'.

It is with a strong feel of déjà vu that the events surrounding the recession and budgetary matters took the shape of embattled politicians of the different parties putting down and ridiculing each other's policies. Hasn't anybody told politicians that every time they open their mouths they reveal their insecurities and self-interests, particularly when they attack the opposition? Politicians' (and not only politicians) lack of intimacy with their own interior landscape and lack of familiarity with how our interiority shapes our choices and behaviours, literally from moment to moment, can lead to a good deal of harm, both to the people governed and to others. It is important that politicians seek to find an inner solidarity from which nobody can demean, lessen or exile them. Belonging is a fundamental human need: people want to belong to a partner, a family, a group, a workplace, a community and a country. However, when adult it is unwise to belong to anything outside yourself; at least, first it is vital to belong to your own unique interiority.

In the battle between the political parties the phrase frequently used is 'politics as usual'. This phrase usually means that people are fairly cynical about politics and politicians, oftentimes understandably so. In the preparation for this article I asked several people for their opinion of the election campaigns. Typical comments were: 'they're all the same'; 'they're all chancers'; 'genuine people don't last in politics'; 'they're only out for themselves'. Maybe what we could wish for with a newly formed government is a politics not as usual, but a wise democracy that exhibits a genuine inquiry into the inner and outer needs of its people and shapes a mature society in which life, liberty and the pursuit of physical, emotional, social, economic and spiritual wellbeing unfold. Of course the genuine needs of a society are always multiple and can sometimes be in conflict with each other for limited resources. The never-ending crisis in the health service bears witness to this fact. However, while a politics grounded in mindfulness of its people may be likely to be still chaotic, contentious and spirited, it would also be one in which the people would be more likely to place their trust. The reality is that people are ultimately trusting in themselves through one another and recognition and honouring of that fact by politicians and other leaders would benefit all, not least the politicians and leaders themselves.

The more mindfulness of self and others becomes a heartfelt practice and priority among politicians, the more there will be an increasing likelihood that politicians will respond to difficult situations in measured, imaginative and powerful ways rather than reacting in the usual defensive ways. I am not advocating some kind of unrealistic perspective. I am referring to the power of honesty and wholeheartedness, and trust in the goodness of all of us radiating through, when it is embodied by those in leadership positions. There is no doubt we would benefit from greater consciousness emanating from our political leaders. But then is it not true to say that we get the politicians we deserve and that any shift towards waking up and coming to our senses will need to unfold across the entire society? This may be the unique challenge for all of us at this time – to respond to the possibilities of our own true nature as human beings, because we can imagine them, because we can know them, and because we see, perhaps as never before, the potential consequences of not being responsible, of not waking up and of not coming to our senses. The fate of human beings and other species may very well hang in the balance, not in some far-off future, but perhaps in the next few generations, much sooner than we think.

4 Quest for Consciousness

Recession: Opportunity for Progression

The word 'recess' has several meanings – a dark cavity in a wall, a break or time-out. The response to the economic recess-ion does not seem to have reflected upon the deeper meanings of the word. There is certainly a frenetic scramble to get back to the prosperity that we had without a consciousness that it has not worked! In terms of the individuals at the top of banks and other financial institutions, no evidence of a deeper reflection and consequential taking responsibility for their reckless actions has emerged. This is true too for many politicians.

There is a need for all of us – not just the bankers, property developers and politicians – to examine the dark inner *recesses* of our minds that led to the collusion with what happened and to the very powerful realities of depersonalisation, avarice, greed, bullying, passivity and superiority that were part and parcel of the well-named 'tiger' economy. In terms of passivity, in the words of Seamus Heaney there was 'the government of the tongue' by heads of work organisations, and the prevailing message among employees was 'whatever you say, say nothing'. Those who allowed themselves to be tongue-tied also need to take responsibility for their non-active response.

Sustained economic prosperity is only possible when there is an equal – I would say greater – focus on the emotional and social prosperity of each individual within our country. The dark development of human resources departments within work organisations led to anonymity at work being a common experience for individual employees. Before the 'boom' these used to be called personnel departments, which largely recognised that it is individual persons that an organisation employed and not a resource to be exploited. Certainly, reflection on the recession needs to involve a very serious look at relationships within the workplace and also relationships with customers which had also become depersonalised. However, a deeper recess within each of us needs to be visited – and that is one's relationship with self.

When any of us confuses self with work, success, wealth, status or power, we bring a dark immaturity to relationships within marriage, family, workplace and community. These addictive responses arose from significant relationships in childhood homes and classrooms and were creatively fashioned as substitutes for the real belonging that is part of our nature – the need for unconditional love. As an adult, it is my responsibility – not optional – to unconditionally belong to self and to operate out from a solid and independent interiority. This is the inner journey that each human being is called upon to travel and there is no better or more fitting time than in the middle of the worst economic crisis that has hit this country; the inner process can bring endless possibilities for a deepening of personal maturity that is critical to emotional, social, political and economic prosperity.

Another issue that needs to be addressed is the belief that the 'tiger' economy was a result of the government emphasis on education from the 1960s onwards. However, a realisation is now needed that education certainly prepared people for work, but *not for maturity*. Indeed, it fostered a dependence on work, success and wealth and, thereby, blocked the emergence of personal maturity. Personal maturity is an essential aspect of professional effectiveness, a reality that hopefully will be realised. The notion too that 'the pen is lighter than the shovel' also demeaned work that is central to physical and social wellbeing. What came about was the importing of labour to do this important work. Education needs to ensure that all work is appreciated and valued and that the pen cannot do without the shovel or the shovel without the pen. The threat that 'you'll end up working on the roads' came from a defensive superiority and has proved to be counterproductive. Education needs to be primarily geared towards individual maturity – an empowering of individuals to take responsibility for self and one's actions. It needs to stay loyal to the true meaning of education (from the Latin word *educare* – meaning to draw out) and work from the inside-out of each individual student. The more educators affirm the unique presence of each student and appreciate the unique creativity and intelligence that each individual student brings to the classroom, the greater likelihood of sustained emotional, social and economic prosperity.

To Question or Not to Question: That is the Question

Life is a mystery; our presence is a mystery and it is highly unlikely that we will ever in one lifetime find all the answers. Indeed, because the universe continues to expand all of the time, the mystery deepens and, so, in many ways will always remain elusive – somewhat like the search for one's own soul, one's deep emotional self. Is it then better not to question; just live for today and not be concerned about the deeper questions? In my opinion it is certainly wise to live for today but I do need to question as if I am going to live forever.

The very fact that a question arises in our minds indicates both a state of *not knowing* and *knowing*. The not knowing is clearly evident but no question could emerge if I already did not have a knowing. To put it another way: you cannot ask a question unless you know that you do not know. To decide not to question – consciously or unconsciously – means you are repressing what you do know about not knowing and repressions always block the emergence of the self and a getting to know and understand the world we live in.

It appears then that the very fact that a question arises indicates, one, that there is a knowing of an unknowing, and, two, a knowing of a possible knowing. Something is prodding you from the inside, saying 'there is something here that you need to know'. When we ignore that inner nudging then personal, interpersonal, societal and spiritual progress is jeopardised. It appears to me that, prior to the recession, either top line managers of the banks and other financial institutions and politicians knew what was going on and did nothing (failed to question) or they did not know what was going on and thereby were not in a mature place to see or question the 'failures' that were occurring. The old saying 'when good men do nothing evil thrives' misses an essential point: that 'good' (meaning 'mature') men will automatically question and know and seek answers when they do not feel competent in their work; they definitely would not turn a blind eye to the recklessness, avarice, greed and narcissism that are now so evident.

There is an urgent need for the individuals that were primarily responsible for the economic crisis to take the time to reflect and to ask the 'how' and 'what' questions: 'how was it that they allowed such a major crisis to develop?' and 'what are the personal, interpersonal and professional actions that they need to take to remedy the situation?' For those who claim that they did not know what was going on, their question is: 'how was it that I was not up to the job I was doing?' and 'what are the things I need to do to increase my personal, interpersonal and professional maturity?' Personal maturity is the foundation of professional effectiveness. Revelations in the banks regarding covering up the truth of the level of debt to NAMA does not auger well for the future, and some of the decisions of the government with regard to cutting costs – for example in relation to respite care for those with intellectually challenged children – are a very real source of concern. I truly wonder whether the person who devised such a cost cutting has been challenged – questioned – on the insensitivity of his decision and I hope that he has been offered the opportunity to reflect on the source of that heartless decision. It does not yet seem to have filtered down into the consciousness of those in possession of considerable economic and political power that societal progress and economic prosperity are dependent on mature emotional and social processes. Money and wealth do not create stability or maturity, but transparency, real responsibility, accountability and management that are both head- and heart-directed do.

The power of a question is that it touches you somewhere within your heart; if it did not touch you, no question would arise. In the light of what has happened over the last three years – religiously, politically and economically – the absence of questions, worryingly and sadly, indicates heartlessness in the actions of people – mostly men – in the carrying out of their responsibilities. When no questions are arising then somehow you are stuck, static, not moving and it can take a crisis to get you back on the enquiry trail and, sometimes, even the crisis fails to bring about that desired effect; when it doesn't – and at the moment it seems very much like that – there are grave reasons to be concerned.

Creating a Better Society

No matter where you are or what you are doing, whether you are alone or with others, you are always in relationship. Typically, we think of relationship in terms of intimate relationships between, for example, lovers or spouses or parent and child. However, different types of relationships occur in all places where individuals live, work, play and pray and these liaisons require as much attention as those relationships between intimates. Indeed, with what has transpired within church, banks, government, public bodies and sporting bodies, there is an urgent need to address the quality of relationships within these social systems. The depersonalisation, narcissism, individualism, cover-ups of abuse, mis-use of taxpayers' monies, greed, cosy circles of deceit and superiority are just some examples of the extreme failures in relationships that have emerged – and the uncovering is not even remotely over. Sadly, it is still the case that the most dangerous place to be is the family. Schools, too, need to address the issue of relationship first, education second, as there are many students who complain of anonymity and teachers who are highly stressed due to an examination-result fixated mentality. The social and economic crises we are currently undergoing here and elsewhere indicate that education has proven to be no reliable index of maturity.

What is frequently missed about the nature of relationship is that each relationship is always a couple relationship and also that each relationship is different to all others. For instance, within the family, each child has a different relationship with each parent and vice versa and the parent who claims to treat all her children in the same way misses this fundamental fact of the uniqueness and creativity of each relationship. Similarly, each student relates to the teacher in a different way and vice versa and it is the mature teacher who recognises that each student responds to his presence and what he says or does in accordance with his or her own unique interiority. It is for this reason that teaching needs to be always focused on the individual and not the group. In the workplace, to our major detriment, where sight has been lost of the critical role of relationship, the reality is that each employee has a different manager and it is the mature manager who is highly conscious of this essential fact. It needs to become the situation that within workplaces – particularly within financial and, ironically, health and social services – individual employees can bring their individuality, creativity, values and beliefs into the workplace and no longer be limited and feel threatened by a target-fixated mentality that puts profit before people and performance before employees' personal wellbeing.

A determining factor of what happens between people is what happens within each member of the dyad. Whether we are conscious or unconscious of this fact, whether we like it or not, each person's inner world – how one perceives self, one's fears, doubts, insecurities, unresolved conflicts or one's fearlessness, belief in self and occupation of an inner stronghold – determines how one perceives and interacts with the other. This is a two-way street and when individuals have little sense of their worth, are dependent, fearful and have had to repress many aspects of their true nature, they are either a danger to themselves or to others, or both. It follows that when individuals have a strong sense of their worth, are stable, mature and tolerant, they create relationships that are of a progressive rather than a defensive nature. Personal effectiveness – a solid interiority – a deep knowing of self – determines professional effectiveness, a fact that needs to be urgently integrated into education and training of professionals so that the recent history of political, religious, economic, social and emotional scandals are not repeated.

In my book, *Relationship, Relationship, Relationship: The Heart of a Mature Society* with co-author Dr Helen Ruddle (2010), all of the above issues are explored in depth. We especially emphasise the responsibility that each and every one of us has to reflect on how we are within ourselves and how, out of that place, we relate to others. If our inner world is harmonious then we will be better able to live with one another in harmony; it is in this sense that individual maturity leads to mature society. For persons who occupy positions of governorship over others, the responsibility of personal maturity is particularly urgent. The recession that has hit the world in recent times can be traced to deep emotional processes where trust had disappeared, where there was little room for individuality, where performance was prized above wellbeing and where there was an overwhelming push for 'success' at all costs.

The book is especially aimed at those adults in our society who have leadership, managerial and parental responsibilities. While aimed at both men and women, the book seeks, in particular, to draw in men who traditionally have not seen relationship as belonging to their sphere of business; we emphasise that for the sake of mature society this is an area that men can no longer afford to avoid.

Is Unconditional Love Possible in the Workplace?

When children do not experience unconditional love in the holding worlds of family, child-minding and pre-primary, primary and post primary schools, inevitably they suffer loss of self-esteem. When their regular relationship experiences are of a conditional nature – 'be good', 'be perfect', 'be quiet',' be hardworking', 'be like me', 'be top of the class', 'be a winner' – they wisely conform or rebel or develop an avoidance strategy against these proscriptions. When they conform they will do all in their power to measure up to the unrealistic expectations because they know that to fall short is to risk the greatest blow of all – harsh rejection or being a disappointment with the consequence of being ignored. Those children who rebel act-out the hurt of their unique presence being confused with a specific behaviour and they equally do all in their power to ensure they get attention, albeit substitute, for being difficult and troublesome. Some children attempt to go under the radar so that the risk of rejection is reduced but, nonetheless, they cleverly get attention for being the 'invisible' child, the one that causes no trouble: 'you'd hardly know he's there'. The wise ploy being employed here is avoidance – 'the less I do the less likely that I'll fail to meet the conditions for recognition' – thereby reducing the risks of being rejected.

What has all the foregoing to do with unconditional love in the workplace? The interesting fact is that employees are categorised under three main headings: those who are 'highly engaged', those who are 'disengaged' and those who are 'CAVE dwellers'. The highly engaged employees are the ones that organisations develop all sorts of reward packages to retain because of their talents, dedication and productivity. When children, these employees were the ones who conformed to parental unrealistic expectations and their dependence continues to be reinforced in the workplace. Their individuality and maturity have been quietly suffocated by conditional recognition for their achievements. The terror of failure continues to dominate their lives and the pressures they put on themselves to perform they also put on others – colleagues and their own children. They are not happy campers and yet, to their own cost and to the cost of others, they often occupy the upper echelons of power – political, work organisational, educational, financial and social. Unless they come to an unconditional acceptance of themselves and an independence from the responses and expectations of others, they will continue to live lives of quiet desperation but also be a threat to the wellbeing of others.

When children, the 'disengaged' employees are the ones who developed the avoidance strategy and they do the least for the most money in the workplace. These employees are difficult to motivate as they tend to go for the average, avoid risk-taking, are passive and fight shy of responsibility – all ways of offsetting criticism and rejection. Unless they free themselves of the fears of failure, of what others think of them and come to an inhabiting of their own individuality and a responsibility for self and their own actions, they will remain hidden under the blanket of avoidance.

The CAVE (constantly against virtually everything) dwellers are the rebels, the troublemakers, the gossips who do little but protest loudly. Their fears of rejection are hidden behind their aggressive and bullying responses. They too hate responsibility and are expert at 'passing the buck'. Sadly, their behaviour alienates others (recognition in itself!) and work organisations will do anything to get them to move out – even paying them off! Redemption for these unhappy individuals also lies in discovering that they are worthy of love for their unique self and that being confused with particular behaviours has been a painful journey.

It appears to me that unconditional recognition is an essential requirement within workplaces and when it is present what is more likely to emerge is a new category of employees – 'engaged' workers – who operate from a solid interiority of independence and deep regard for self and others and who view work as love made visible. These mature employees will integrate work as an important part of their lives and they will bring the fullness of their commitment, intelligence, creativity and affectivity to the workplace.

In the words of the late John O'Donohue (1999), 'it is futile to weary your life with the politics of fashioning a persona in order to meet the expectations of other people' and in my words, 'it is a protection to hide yourself away in order to avoid the rejection of others and what a disaster not to be found.' Without unconditional love no safety to be self and no maturity is present. Unconditional regard is not a 'soft' issue as many managers who are in fearful places believe; indeed, it is the 'hardest' challenge of all. The 'success' (highly engaged) culture that emerged in the last two decades has not served us well; it was and still is characterised by depersonalisation, greed, individualism, insensitivity and a lack of accountability and authenticity. Individuality, authenticity and accountability are the essential bases for emotional, social, spiritual and economic prosperity; however, these necessary qualities are only possible in a climate of unconditional recognition in places where we live, learn, work, play and pray. In the presence of the current dark economic and political fallouts and the denial evident in the Catholic hierarchy, the urgency to address unconditional love has been never more pressing.

Is Compassion Possible in the Workplace?

Compassion is an emotion that arises in response to understanding that the difficult behaviours of either employees or managers are not consciously deliberate in their neglect of others but are unconsciously designed to bring attention to the individual's inner turmoil. Is it a bridge too far to ask an employee who has been relentlessly bullied by a manager to have a compassionate understanding of the manager's unconscious plight? Such a situation is only possible when individuals who have been bullied first of all develop a compassionate understanding of their own emotional pain and the passivity that has unconsciously prevented the emergence of an assertiveness that would have challenged the bullying behaviour when it first presented. There are two very separate issues that require consideration here – one, the plight of those who are at the receiving end of bullying and two, the plight of those who, owing to their inner insecurities, resort to bullying to reduce perceived threats to their wellbeing. There is a further consideration – that compassionate understanding is suggesting that individuals who bully or who are passive are responsible *to* their defensive responses but they are not responsible *for* their actions. The 'to' and 'for' distinction is important because when others insist you are 'responsible for' your actions, they are judging that you are deliberately being neglectful, whereas when others assert the need for you to take 'responsibility *to*' your actions, they know that your bullying arises from a place of hurt within yourself; in this way they are compassionate and non-judgemental but still assert the need for you to take responsibility to the neglect perpetrated.

Returning to the issue of passivity and bullying, being totally separate issues it is imperative that it be understood that individuals who created passivity as a powerful means of reducing hurt *never invite* others to bully them. People who bully do so because of their own inner turmoil and the reason why they appear to bully only those who are passive is because it would not have worked with those who are assertive. Indeed, their unconscious strategy will be to do all in their power to *avoid* (another defensive strategy) those who are assertive because at a deep level they know that their insecurities will be spotted by those who act from an inner stronghold.

The challenging issue is that no progress can be made unless somebody – preferably a person in a key management position – views the untenable situation with compassionate understanding. It is this person who can attempt to ensure that the person doing the bullying is provided with the emotional and social safety for whatever unconscious insecurity to come to consciousness so that he can be accountable for his threatening actions, by taking due responsibility and making recompense. When compassionate understanding is not present, the person who bullies will continue to do so and may be quite vehement that the rest of the world is out of step and that he has no problem. In a similar vein the persons who are at the receiving end of the intimidating behaviour will continue to judge the person doing the bullying and will not come to realise their own defensive position of passivity. The key mature person will also create the opportunities for those who have been passive to become empowered so that the early experiences of being threatened are reported as soon as it happens. Of course, the latter depends upon the employee feeling that it is safe to report bullying and that decisive action will be taken to restore workplace wellbeing. The difficulty is that such safety has not been present and that those further up the line in management are often more intimidating than those in the lower and middle management group. Those who head work organisations need to closely examine their level of maturity, but it is often the case that they too are as unconsciously imprisoned by their insecurities. What hope then is there for progress? What inevitably will emerge are major crises within the organisation and the hope is that such conflict will lead to mature help being sought *outside* for what has become a dark and threatening work organisation. The fall of the banks, other financial institutions, the property developers, the church and a heavily besieged government are examples of these 'inevitable' crises. However, there is not much evidence yet that an authentic examination is taking place by organisational heads of their insecurities, work relationships and work practices. If this does not emerge then the crises necessarily need to deepen in order to 'wake up' those who hold the reins of power to take hold of the reins of maturity.

Emotions Call for Motion

Emotions arise spontaneously and accurately mirror your interior world at that moment in time. Emergency feelings emerge in response to perceived threats to your wellbeing – the word 'perceived' meaning that what determines each person's response to an emotional, sexual, physical, intellectual or social threat is the level of security felt within. In other words, one person's emotional response to the same criticism can be totally different to another's. This latter phenomenon is very evident in workplaces where a manager's shouting affects each employee differently. This shows that each employee's unique response is a function of his or her level of emotional security and that the manager's shouting, while always threatening in nature to staff members' wellbeing, is not the direct cause of a particular employee's response. It is paramount that the manager examines what is within him that is giving rise to his shouting and to take responsibility to resolve that inner turmoil. It is equally crucial to examine each employee's emotional reaction – particularly those who feel most distressed – so that the person can be more empowered to withstand the manager's threatening behaviour. The most important question to ask the employee is: what do you feel when the manager shouts? Similarly, the manager needs to be asked the question: what are you feeling when you start shouting? Feelings are our most accurate barometer and are designed to alert to the threats that are present, to the fearfulness within and to the need for resolution.

The distinction between emergency and welfare feelings is an important one. Emergency emotions – for example fear, anger, sadness, guilt, jealousy, disgust – alert to the reality that there is some relationship emergency happening and a need to take action in the face of the present threat to wellbeing. When the person at the receiving end of the threatening behaviour is quite solid and secure, the emergency feeling will prompt an assertive safe-guarding action to reduce or eliminate the threat. For example, if your boss reads you the riot act in front of your colleagues, you will respond quite definitely: 'John, two things: one, when you need to talk to me about an issue that is upsetting you, please do so with me in private and two, talk about what unmet needs you have rather than being verbally aggressive.' This is a rare response; the more common response is to feel angry, put down, humiliated, and either to attack back or swallow down what you are feeling and passively take the verbal tirade or get up and remove yourself from the scene. When you passively remove yourself from the scene, you are revealing on how you are removed from respect and care for self. Equally, when you attack back or later gossip maliciously about your boss, you are in a disconnected place within. Whatever the defensive response, there is urgency for you to find the support to reclaim that care of self so that the threat-ening responses of others are no longer tolerated by you. In asserting boundaries around your dignity, be sure you do not become a source of threat to another.

All emergency emotions are created to move you in the direction of wellbeing. However, when you are operating from an inner place of fearfulness, necessarily your response to emergency feelings will be to blame self or another, or to dilute, neutralize, displace, modify or suppress as follows:

- Blame self – 'I'm so pathetic'
- Blame another – 'You make me angry'
- Dilute – 'It's not as bad as I think it is'
- Neutralise – 'What I'm feeling is no different to anybody else'
- Displace – 'The house is driving me crazy' or 'It's probably due to something that I ate'
- Modify – 'I'm not really feeling depressed; probably just a little down in myself'
- Suppress – 'What I'm feeling is ridiculous; I'm just going to ignore it.'

All the above defensive responses will result in the emergency feeling increasing in frequency, intensity and endurance in order to bring attention to the *real* movement that is being called for. It is critical that the person seeks support and help to take the authentic actions to bring about feelings of wellbeing. When welfare feelings – joy, love, confidence, aliveness, enthusiasm – become the more frequent and persistent feelings, then the emergency feelings have achieved their goal.

The Power of Anger

Buddhism is being explored by many Irish people as an alternative to a Catholicism that, sadly, lost its spiritual way a long time ago. While there are many aspects of Buddhism that I find myself drawn to, I do have difficulty with its understanding of anger. The Dalai Lama, the exiled spiritual leader of Tibet, is quoted as saying: 'Cut off all anger.' He believes that anger is too dangerous to fool around with. He encourages people to 'rid yourself of it for the benefit of all sentient beings'.

He also asserts that 'if anger comes into the mind, it will also come into the mouth'.

The rise of anger management courses also suggests that anger is bad and needs to be controlled. However, I believe that both

Buddhism and some psychological approaches confuse anger with aggression. Anger is a feeling; it cannot hurt anyone. Aggression is an action – verbal, written, physical – that can certainly hurt others. Considerable human pain is caused by the mightiest weapon of all – the tongue. Hostile criticism, ridicule, scoldings, 'put down' messages, sarcasm, cynicism, comparisons are some examples of verbal and written aggression that cause much human hurt and suffering. Physical violence that utterly demeans or annihilates the presence of those who are at the receiving end is still very much with us in Irish society.

It is not anger that gives rise to aggression – that which comes into the mouth – but the non-ownership of it. Anger is an e-motion; its purpose is to move the person who feels anger to take action for self on the blocked need or violated value to which anger is drawing attention. Anger creates the energy that is required to move us into championing ourselves or others. Without anger we would not have the power to stand up for what is fair, loving and respectful. Injustices and neglects that occur within the social systems of family, school, community and workplace would go unchallenged were anger to be got rid of. The essential message in anger is to take action *for* self or others, not action *against*. When the action is against someone, there may be judgement, harshness, dismissal, hostility and lessening of another person's presence. This then is aggression, not anger.

Anger, next to love, is our most valued emotion. Aggression (not anger) management needs to focus on helping individuals to understand the true nature of anger and how to employ it constructively. When anger arises, a number of responses are required so that it remains the property of the person feeling it and does not get projected onto others:

- value its presence
- own it as a message to you and for you
- detect the blocked or violated need or right
- determine the action needed to get the need met or to restore the violated need
- take the required verbal or physical self-action.

Typically, anger arises when another person judges you, for example as 'useless', 'selfish' or 'uncaring'. Anger arises to alert you to the threat to your presence and it is not too difficult to isolate the violated right – your right to respect. It is not your place to correct the aggressive behaviour of the other person, but it is your place to assert your own worthiness. The assertion may take the form of, 'John, I do not perceive myself in these terms, but I am wondering what blocked need of yours lies behind your judgement of me?' John may react unfavourably but your next action is to say 'John, I am willing to listen to you when you're in a place to communicate respectfully, but right now I am removing myself from your defensiveness.'

The wisdom of anger is very much in evidence when we witness a child being berated or violated in any way. Children need for adults to champion their worthiness and their right to physical, sexual, emotional, intellectual, behavioural, social and creative safety. The purpose of anger in those who witness children being violated is to get them to take action to vindicate the rights of the child and to restore any violated right. This needs to be done in a way that is assertive and definite, but not aggressive and coercive. When it is the latter it is akin to fighting fire with fire and no resolution is now possible. Regrettably, many children are not championed either because the adults who have charge of them are passive (don't use their anger) or aggressive (don't own their anger).

Guilt Trip

A 'guilt trip' is either a journey you create within yourself or one that another person attempts to arrange for you. The person who expects you to take responsibility for him can lay out the terms of the trip with such phrases as 'you only think about yourself'; 'you're never there when I need you'; 'everything else comes first before me' and, even more alarming, 'I am nothing without you'. The latter response is particularly worrying as it may be a precursor to a future losing of all sense of one's value following the break-up of the relationship.

This is not uncommon among young men who either threaten to or do take their own lives following what they interpret as rejection of them by the young woman who ends the relationship. When a person internalises the dependency verbalisations and helpless body and facial expression of another, they will experience guilt. The tendency is to interpret the guilt as about 'letting the other person down'. This reaction is quite common between adult children and their parents and is echoed in such statements as 'I feel so guilty that I haven't rung my mother' (or father) or 'I'm such a bad person for not visiting my parents'. However, when you interpret guilt as your being responsible for the wellbeing of another, you are cleverly avoiding a deeper issue that requires resolution. I know several adults who religiously ring their parents on a twice daily basis and call 'home' two or three times weekly, even though the response they constantly get is critical, cold, heartless and dismissive. Of course, if they dared not ring or turn up, the result would be total silent treatment and a reporting of their 'heartless' behaviour to all other members of the family. In the face of such threats – which have persisted since childhood – seeing guilt as letting the other down is a wise and protective strategy. The wisdom is that by projecting the guilt you now make even greater efforts to look after the person who is demanding and controlling of you, all in an attempt to reduce the ever-present threat of utter rejection.

However, as an adult I need to find the help and support to separate out from a parent (or partner, manager, friend) who leans on me. The protective response was to conform and thereby create a co-dependency and lean-to relationship. The mature response is to take responsibility for your own life and return responsibility for his or her own life to the person who depends on you. This separating out, this taking responsibility for self and your own actions, is an act of love and care both for yourself and for the other. As long as we maintain a co-dependence, then the mature progress of both parties to the relationship is seriously blocked. Feelings of guilt over your behaviour towards another arise from fear of rejection; this fear of rejection can only be resolved through an enduring unconditional love and acceptance of yourself. When you reach that place of solid interiority then you are in that separate place to see that the dependency behaviour of another is about their hidden fears and only they can resolve those deep-seated insecurities. Collusion with another's dependency needs maintains their fears and insecurities.

What is interesting is that when you begin to find space between yourself and the dependent parent, partner, friend or manager, you will then embrace guilt as a messenger of 'how you let yourself down' and the need for you to take responsibility for yourself, not for another. Only when we are independent are we truly in a place to love and empower another to come home to their inner stronghold. The hope is that once one party to the lean-to relationship moves towards independence, the other may take his or her cue from that modelling of maturity and set forth themselves on the road to a recovery of their true self. Whether or not this mature process ensues, there can be no going back for the person who is now travelling the road less travelled – free from guilt and responsible for self.

Mining the Diamond

There are individuals who have been so traumatised when they were minors and continue to be re-traumatised in their later and current years that they necessarily and creatively have buried their true self and their true nature in the dark subterranean world of the unconscious – very akin to the Chilean miners who found themselves buried for sixty-nine days 600 metres below ground level. Not only did each of the thirty-three miners have to face the demon mountain that had collapsed in on top of them but it is now becoming apparent that each of them also had to face his own inner demons. The demons each one of us have had to face are the mis-takes made by parents and other significant adults when they confused our presence with our behaviour and the continuation of the sanctification of those mistakes in schools, classrooms, communities, churches and workplaces. When a child is not responded to unconditionally, when his person is not seen as separate from his behaviour and when certain behaviours gain attention and others rejection, then it is like extinguishing the light of a candle with one movement and plunging the child into utter and relentless darkness. Another way of describing this sad phenomenon is that having one's individuality completely ignored or harshly rejected or conditionally accepted is like being pushed quite out of life – like being blown out as one blows out a candle. Clearly the frequency of the extinctions, the intensity of the responses and the endurance over time add immeasurably to the darkness.

If after sixty-nine days the Chilean miners were wonderfully rescued from what initially was seen as certain death, individuals who have had to bury the light of their unique worth from early childhood can be trapped down in their subterranean dark havens for years on end without any signs of being rescued. I call these heartless places havens because the individuals know that any attempt to move towards expressing their light will result in further annihilation and so there is a comfort in being hidden, but what a tragedy if they are never found! What was striking about the Chilean rescue mission was the presence of love, patience, determination and ingenuity to bring the trapped men to the surface. These same qualities are needed to rescue individuals who feel that nobody is ever going to see their lovability and the preciousness of their unique lives.

Like the Chilean miners who fought against tremendous odds to keep their spirits alive – particularly when there had been no contact from the outside for seventeen days – and who fervently hoped to be saved, individuals in psychological darkness also crave redemption. Having been delivered from their underground prison, the Chilean miners still had to face their own inner demons, which I have no doubt came very much to the forefront when they encountered the mining disaster. Facing these inner demons – the darkness of not being loved and cherished for self – takes far longer than sixty-nine days, but the hope is that the love, courage and endurance shown by their rescuers, family members, lovers and friends – even politicians – provided the safety for each of them to go on his own much more hazardous inner rescue mission. What would help enormously is the continuation of the tremendous support shown during their time when they were trapped in the dark bowels of the San Jose mine.

Each of us has mining of the unique diamond of self to do – there is not one of us who does not have self-esteem difficulties. While it is the responsibility of each one of us to inhabit his or her own individuality, it is also the responsibility of each of us to provide the love, patience, kindness, support and encouragement that creates the safety for the person hidden in heartless darkness to reveal and express his or her fullness. Of course, the tragedy is that in order to possess such qualities one would have needed to have plumbed the depths of one's own pain and be able then to sit with the pain of another. If it takes the world to raise a child it also takes the world to rescue individuals from the darkness of anonymity. The Chilean miners' story is a lesson for all of us but we need to realise that the person sitting across from you right now or your own self may be locked away in miserable and hopeless darkness and are we in a place to stretch out a helping hand?

The New Profession of Relationship Mentoring

Whatever relationship you have, it is *always* a couple relationship – whether this is a parent with child, a lover with a lover, a teacher with a student, a manager with an employee, a politician with a citizen, a priest with a parishioner, a neighbour with a neighbour. Each couple relationship is unique so that each child has a different mother and a different father; each student has a different teacher, each employee a different manager, each parishioner a different priest, and so on for all relationships.

What is often not recognised is that the most important couple relationship is the one that a person has with self and, indeed, the nature of that inner relationship totally determines how that person relates to another. It follows that a person who doubts or hates self, is dependent on others for recognition, is obsessed with what others think of him, is addicted to food, alcohol or success or is aggressive, passive, unsure, timid or fearful will create a relationship with another that in some way or other reflects that person's inner relationship with self.

Individuals who head the important places where we live, work, learn, pray, heal and play, depending on their inner relationship with self, can create harmony or wreak havoc in their relationships with others. Regrettably, the relationship record of some of these heads leaves a lot to be desired, and this has become so visible since the sexual abuse revelations and cover-ups by Catholic clergy and the appalling levels of irresponsibility shown by politicians, public servants, bankers, heads of other financial institutions and multinational companies and property developers. Even before the recession, a large majority of people who moved on to other jobs did so because of the intimidating behaviour of managers. There is no attempt here to blame these heads; on the contrary, no progress can be made unless we get to understand what led individual members of Catholic clergy to sexually violate children and other leading clergy to cover up these same violations. What were the influences that saw individual politicians, public servants, bankers and other heads mentioned above lining their own pockets without any ethical consideration being present?

It behoves all heads – parents, teachers, managers, politicians, sports leaders, health care professionals and clergy – to examine their inner worlds and to resolve whatever blocks to maturity exist therein. The answers lie in relationship and the stories of the important relationships those heads have had to date. It is a sad reality that a family is where most neglect occurs, a school is a place you can't wait to leave, a workplace that you can literally feel sick at the thought of, a church where you feel invisible or a country where you feel alienated. The question arises: who is going to support and help these heads (and, indeed, the rest of us) to examine our inner and outer lives, in an understanding and compassionate way, to bring to consciousness the repressions of aspects of our true nature that led to the great neglects perpetrated.

Help is at hand in the emergence of the new professions of parent mentoring and relationship mentoring. The highly trained practitioners work on both a one-to-one basis with heads of familial, social, religious, educational and economic systems, but also provide intensive training courses for groups of individuals – heads and members – who occupy the systems.

The professional training of these mentors involved principally examining their own inner and outer lives and the making of new choices and taking new actions when consciousness of their own hidden issues arose. Parent mentors undertake a two-year training course and relationship mentors complete up to four years training. These mentors know what the ingredients of mature relationships are and how relationships in all the different life settings can be seriously interrupted. They are well aware that *affectiveness* is critical to the resolution of interruptions. They can readily detect whether or not listening occurs and whether or not communication is open, direct and clear and whether or not definite boundaries around each individual's wellbeing are in place. Most of all, the mentors know that it is the nature of the relationship with self that is the bedrock of personal maturity and the maturity of relationships with others. The mentors are trained to create a relational depth that makes it emotionally, intellectually, socially, behaviourally and creatively safe for the person(s) seeking help to explore their relationships to date and to see what needs to be seen and to do what needs to be done – for the benefit of all.

5 People-Managing with Consciousness

Management Without Relationship

One of the most frequent complaints of employees is of anonymity in the workplace. Coupled with that experience is that at least one in four employees regularly experiences bullying and eighty per cent do so intermittently. Certainly, the government has recognised this reality by insisting on anti-bullying policies within workplaces, but these regulations do not appear to be having any significant effect. A deeper inquiry is required to establish why so many managers bully. I am quite sure that such aggressive behaviour arises from fear. The nature and causes of that fear will differ for each manager who engages in bullying and, as such, the resolution of bullying lies with the individual.

Management is one of the most common professions around and at its best it is less than mediocre. There appears to be a very counterproductive belief in work organisations that management has nothing to do with the happiness and wellbeing of workers; it is viewed as a mechanical rather than an emotional and social process. Mechanical management can lead to the commoditising of employees and this is powerfully seen in the use of such derogatory terms as 'human resources', 'human capital' and 'staff retention'. There appears to be little or no recognition of the emotional reality that human beings want to belong – to a partner, a family, a community, a classroom, a school or the workplace. To ignore this innate need to belong creates a dark ethos within any social system, including the workplace. Certainly, it is the responsibility of each adult to belong to self and never belong totally to anything outside self. Rumi, the Sufi poet, puts it so well when he says, 'A person only becomes an adult when he takes responsibility for self and for his own actions.' Such maturity is essential for managers; how else can they manage employees effectively and affectively? Management is essentially both a head and heart phenomenon. The absence of the heart qualities in many males can lead them 'to lose their heads' more easily. Equally, the absence of head qualities in females can lead them 'to lose their hearts' more easily and resort to passivity.

It is a serious neglect of managers themselves and employees to not provide potential managers with the opportunities to examine their level of maturity – the extent to which they know and belong to self. It puzzles me why it is only psychotherapists and psychoanalysts who are required to examine their lives. There is recognition in that requirement that unless therapists have resolved or at least are on the way to consciously resolving their own conflicts, they are not in a mature place to help others. But surely the professions of parenting, teaching, management, medicine, psychiatry, social work, politics – all of which have major influence on the lives of those for whom they have a responsibility of care – need to examine their current level of maturity. It is important to know that age, gender, education, wealth, status and power are no indices of maturity. It is now well documented that parents can only bring children to the same level of development and maturity they have reached themselves – but, of course, this is also true for all the other professions in terms of the individuals for which they have a duty of care. When maturity is not present, great neglect can occur, and this can be and is so evident in the political arena.

When it comes to the training of managers, it appears we are still in the dark ages. Management is primarily about relationship – the enhancement of relationships, the enrolling of cooperation and the enabling and empowering of employees. It seems such a simple truth to say that an employee who has a sense of belonging and who is happy and contented is the most valuable asset to any work organisation. However, this reality can only be appreciated by the individuals in charge of organisations who belong to self and are not unhealthily enmeshed with power, status, wealth or success and who do not have a target-fixated mentality. Training in management needs to include an examination of the manager's interiority and the provision of the opportunities to move towards a solid interiority – what I like to call an inner stronghold – from which he can manage employees in a way that dignifies their presence and creates an environment where it is a joy to come to work. Such a manager is an invaluable asset to any work organisation, but it is only the enlightened leaders of work organisations that will appreciate such maturity. In many ways, work organisations get the managers they deserve. In situations where mature management is not appreciated, employees may have difficult decisions to make. Ideally, work and workplace need to be always worthy of each employee's dignity.

The End to Insensitivity

On a recent reading of the business section of one of Ireland's national newspapers I came across a column titled 'Why insensitivity is a vital managerial trait.' I hesitated before reading the article and checked to see whether the date was April 1st! After all, given the shocking betrayals revealed about heads within the Church, the banks, other financial institutions, government bodies and the Gardaí, it seems quite perverse of any writer to be in praise of insensitivity. Not only have the leaders and managers of those various institutions mentioned lost the trust of their heretofore followers, but there is a boiling anger and even rage brewing about their heartless conduct. The major problem with the management of our leading economic, social, political and religious organisations has been a depersonalisation of individuals, an avarice, greed, superiority, arrogance and, as yet, refusal to take responsibility for their inhumanity to man.

What gave rise to the article was the declaration by Jon Moulton, founder and managing partner of the private-equity firm Alchemy, of his three strongest character traits: determination, curiosity and insensitivity. In the words of Jon Moulton, 'the great thing about insensitivity is that it lets you sleep when others can't.' One wonders who are 'the others' he is referring to – are they the ones at the receiving end of his insensitivity and seething with rage at being an anonymity within the workforce? How can any mature manager believe that being heartless is going to increase staff loyalty, motivation, productivity, creativity and commitment? Bullying – a product of insensitivity – is a time bomb still waiting to go off in many workplaces.

The writer of the column suggests that being in management means having the ability to take decisions that will hurt individual people. Has the writer any clue that it is the truth that sets people free and that a genuine telling of what are the bases for a difficult decision considerably softens the blow and means that both manager and employee can sleep that night! There have been cases where the insensitive firing of an individual employee has resulted in that employee either returning to shoot the manager and his cohorts or taking his own life, or both. Management is both a head and a heart practice, and management that has head but no heart is not management at all. Equally, management that has heart but no head is not management at all. Effective management is a function of a solid interiority from which nobody can distance, exile, demean or lessen your presence. Sensitivity or being emotionally mature does not mean taking responsibility for others, but it does mean being responsible for self, ensuring that work, wealth, status and power are not tied to one's worth and confidence and that interactions with employees are of a nature that individualises and dignifies their presence. Emotional maturity is also about seeing beyond oneself from an inner stronghold; it does not mean, as the writer of the column suggested, taking what others say personally and staying awake all night agitating on the hurts experienced or witnessed. On the contrary, the mature manager sleeps because he *does* care, does have heart, does affirm the presence of workers, does firmly and authoritatively speak the truth and exercises his responsibility with due care of self, employees, clients, shareholders and the organisation.

Feelings occur spontaneously – they are not consciously manufactured – and they arise with the mature purpose of calling for progressive action. The manager who suppresses or, even worse, represses or denies emotional realities within self and others is a danger to the wellbeing of himself, partner, family and employees and a poor servant of shareholders.

Managers who are fully in touch and expressive of the totality of their nature do not dither or prevaricate but are definite in their decision-making while maintaining a respectful connection with individual employees. My hope is that the days are over of managers who are insensitive, who bully, who depersonalise and who are narcissistic, avaricious, greedy and intimidating. The preference is that these managers will recognise their need to examine their largely unlived lives and seek the necessary help to resolve their insensitivity. However, other members of work and other occupational, social, religious and political organisations cannot afford to wait for managers to transform themselves. It is the responsibility of each of us to understand ourselves and to take due responsibility to transform ourselves and that includes challenging any heartless responses of managers and leaders.

Lean-to Relationships

The more common reality in relationships is co-dependence between the two parties involved; a mutual leaning on one another for a sense of security. Many of us emerge from childhood having learned that to be independent and self-realised is highly dangerous both emotionally and socially; cleverly, we conformed to the projections of the adults in our lives – we either leaned on them or allowed them to lean on us. In protecting ourselves from the threats of rejection, criticism, ridicule, even violence, we unconsciously fashioned a persona that primarily operated from the outside-in rather than from the inner stronghold of the inside-out. We necessarily conformed to the dependent behaviours of our parents, teachers and other significant adults and, sometimes, we rebelled – conformity and rebelliousness being opposite sides of the same coin of dependence. Conformity – the development of a false form, a con-form – means that the self masks its true and powerful nature and goes about the business of people-pleasing. Rebelliousness, on the other hand, is also a false form; its purpose being to counter-control those who are attempting to impose their dependence on you. Rebelliousness also operates from the outside-in because it attempts to get others to conform to your ways. Indeed, both conformity and rebelliousness operate from the place of 'you' – 'you're right' and 'you're wrong'. Maturity operates from the place of 'I' and does not attempt to appease or control others; it takes responsibility for self and all expressions of self and is open to listening to others and giving due consideration to what they are expressing while keeping the final decision for self.

Leaning on others or on achievements or on wealth or success or on the body beautiful creates a profound level of uncertainty – an uncertainty that necessarily tugs at us emotionally because we are out of touch with our true nature which is our basic oneness, our basic unconditional worth and lovability (our al-one-ness). When we lean on others either in explicit, implicit or obscure ways, we expect others to supply what we have hidden about ourselves – strength, security, intelligence, direction, even life itself – and when our expectations are not met we go further off-centre. Leaning on others, we tend to interpret any signs of unavailability or inattention as a rejection or a defeat mirroring earlier such experiences; we re-experience the pain of not being able to conquer the hearts and minds of our parents through our unique presence.

Individuals who are dependent will tend to rubbish any attempts to get them to stand on their own two feet, but they do this because they know too well, albeit unconsciously, the hazards of being independent, of being an individual, of being separate. People who are dependent have not had the safety to enjoy the peace and power of their own solitude – this runs contrary to their story of enmeshment with others. Indeed, they can sometimes be overwhelmed by the unbearable fear of aloneness.

It is a major challenge to create environments – within homes, schools, churches, communities, workplaces, social systems – that provide the safety for members of these holding worlds to be themselves, to self-reveal and to live out their own individual lives. The difficulty is that often the individuals who are in leadership and managerial positions do not inhabit their own individuality and do not model maturity. I believe the focus needs to be on these people because if those in charge do not resolve their dependence, it is very frightening for those who are their charges to challenge their immaturity. The alternatives are either to conform or rebel. Other people are not responsible *for* us but they certainly have responsibilities *to* us – the key responsibility being to not bring their insecurities to our door. We are all fundamentally on our own, and even though this is a natural state – the acceptance of which releases hidden creative resources – it can be a hard fact to take on board because of the threats to independence that exist for all of us, adults as well as children. All human systems – familial, social, economic, educational, legal, political and religious – stand to gain enormously from the modelling, encouragement, support and practice of self-realisation and the inhabiting of individuality by each person, most especially those who govern these systems.

Who Knows You?

I have said it many times that everyone wants to belong. We want to belong to a partner, a family, a group, a workplace, a community. I have also said that the priority is to belong to self, to your own interiority. Otherwise there is a danger of an over-involvement or an under-involvement or no involvement in your relationships with others. Basically the nature of your relationship with another is totally determined by the nature of your relationship with self.

Involvement is about letting another person know you; it is not about the other knowing you! Any person that says 'I know you so well' or 'I know what's best for you' or 'You don't know yourself as I know you' needs to seriously examine such superiority. Nobody can know you better than yourself. Furthermore, another person can only know you to the extent and depth that you let them into your inner world.

Similarly, when a person expects another person to know them and to read their mind, they are not taking on the responsibility to know self. What they are doing is finding a substitute way of knowing self by passing that responsibility onto another. It happens typically in long-term couple relationships where one or other partner, following a situation where expectations have not been met, complains, 'You should know me and what I want after all these years.' Actually, it is not your partner's responsibility to know you, but it is yours! Certainly, it is a bonus when your partner anticipates your needs, but, ultimately, it is up to each of us to communicate our needs to a partner or anybody else.

Lao Tzu, the Chinese sage, says that 'to know self is wise, to know another is learned'. However, I can only learn about another person to the extent of what he or she chooses to reveal about self. You might say, 'Surely you can know a person from their non-verbal language, their verbal responses and their actions?' The reality is that all of these are symptomatic of underlying or hidden issues that another person can have no knowledge of unless the person invites you into their inner terrain. You can certainly guess, make assumptions and have hypotheses, but it is the mature person who verifies these possibilities with the other person.

When I attend social functions some individuals can be quite wary of me, in case, as some say, 'you'll see through me'. Others express a curiosity and want me to analyse them and tell them what kind of personality they have. They are disappointed when I say that I do not have that kind of power. However, I do understand that they may be attempting to 'pass the buck' to me to examine their lives, but, again, this is my hypothesis and I need to check out if that is the case.

Any parent, teacher, partner, lover, friend, therapist, trainer, employer, manager or priest who judges, labels, advises or dismisses your point of view is not operating from a place of solid interiority. Why precisely they are acting in an apparently arrogant and superior way I cannot say, but it would be wise for them to examine what it is that leads them to believe that they can know another person better than the person knows himself or herself. The person at the receiving end of their projections needs to return to them their judgements, labels, advice or dismissal and request that they reflect on the hidden source of these behaviours and the opportunities for consciousness being presented to them.

What about the person who is in denial? Is it not the case that he should be made aware of his irresponsible actions and an insistence made that he examines what lies behind such actions and the threats they pose to others? A typical example of this is how dependence on alcohol can be a major threat to the person's own health and the wellbeing of spouse, children, family of origin, work colleagues and neighbours. Does the person not need a good dose of reality to wake him up to his distressing behaviours? The answer is 'certainly', except that this judgemental and superior approach does not work. There is a therapy in America called KITA (which means 'kick in the ass') which makes no sense to me, because people who are troubled have been hurt enough already. It is a bit like kicking somebody when they are down. The reality is that those professionals who claim the person is in denial cannot know the source of such a powerful defensive behaviour, which was created in the unconscious realm of the mind to protect the person from re-experiencing some tremendous hurts. It is a case of adding insult to injury to tell a person that they have to face up to the reality of their troubled behaviours and act responsibly. There is an implicit assumption that the person wants to stay in the darkness of denial and not come into the light of self-realisation and responsibility for self and towards others. It is my experience that no person wants to stay stuck in the dark tunnel of denial. It is also my experience that a person who is deeply defensive unconsciously knows the great dangers he would face were he to express his buried pain and the truth of what happened to him in his earlier years. We sometimes see that when an adult in a family reveals being sexually abused by a parent, all the other family members reject him or her for being authentic.

Revolutions and Inner Resolutions

The wellbeing of all relationships depends on the depth, breadth and maturity of the inner relationship that each person has with self. All social systems – family, schools, classrooms, societies, clubs, workplaces, churches, communities – are a collective of individuals and what each person brings to a social system in terms of maturity, knowledge, skills, values and beliefs will determine the ethos of the particular system of which he or she is a member. Social systems and societies do not change, but when individuals change, society is influenced. Leadership is a crucial agent of the wellbeing of a social system. It is for this reason we talk about parents being the architects of the family culture, teachers the architects of the classroom atmosphere, managers the architects of the staff ethos, political leaders the architects of a country's wellbeing and so on. There is no suggestion here that leaders and managers take all the responsibility for the welfare of the group, but they do need to be aware that people take their cues from the ways they are with others. It is for this reason that a leader who is antagonistic, irritable, critical and dominating is likely to experience fear, passivity, no risk-taking among the staff group or an aggressive challenging of his actions. It is not that the members are sheep-like, but they know the dangers of rocking the boat and so they take up a defensive stance, particularly if they are unsure of themselves. The person who is mature and self-possessed will not tolerate a bullying-type leadership and will assertively challenge (as opposed to defensively) the threatening responses of the person in charge. The person who is mature will not compromise his dignity for the sake of employment. Sadly, there are many family, work and religious organisations that do not embrace the member who is self-actualised. A friend of mine was recently described as 'over-self-developed for this work organisation' by an evaluating consultancy team hired by her work organisation!

The reality is that there is no person without some emotional baggage. The heavier the emotional baggage, the greater the threat you are to your own wellbeing and the wellbeing of others.

Emotional baggage represents all the parts of yourself that you have repressed or suppressed from early on in childhood. Those aspects of self we dare not show are defended by behaviours that sadly become a threat to the welfare of others – such as aggression, passivity, cynicism, violence, sarcasm, blaming, avoiding responsibilities, threats, sexual violation, competitiveness, addictions (to alcohol, drugs, work), anxiety, dread and timidity.

It is ironic that in a so-called civilised society we do not create opportunities, support, encouragement and resources for the most important relationship of all – the relationship with self. The wonderful paradox is that the more you know, love and appreciate your own unique self, the less selfish and controlling you become. The relationship with self is not a narcissistic pursuit as some people defensively claim. On the contrary, the relationship with self is about taking responsibility for all aspects of self – physical, sexual, emotional, intellectual, behavioural, social, creative and spiritual. On the other hand, narcissism is about 'me, me, me' and the attempt to get everyone to revolve around you, including the world. The person who engages in narcissism has often been 'spoilt' as a child and had parents who danced attention on him or her. The child intuitively senses his parents' need to live their lives through him and so, wisely, suppresses his right to live his own life and take responsibility for same. It is the wise parent who knows that parenting is as much about enabling children to take responsibility for themselves as it is about loving them for their unique selves. This attitude needs to be part and parcel of all leadership.

The path to freeing ourselves from our emotional baggage is not easy, but it is essential; otherwise we buy ourselves a life of misery and can be a source of considerable misery to others.

What better time than now to begin to make the resolution to deepen your relationship with self. Be wary that there will be many who walk the well-trodden path of dependence who will do all in their power to block you travelling the path less travelled. Find people who will support your inner process and realise that those who are threatened by your determination to know self, deep down behind their defensive behaviours, wish to be free as well. Indeed, you may well become the leader and provide support for them to begin the process of inner revolution.

There are many ways to start on the road – loving kindness towards self being the most important. However, the freedom to love self may be hidden behind thick walls of defences and it is risky to forego this pseudo-comfort zone. Start with little kindnesses and persist with them. Remind yourself that in the same way that each child deserves love, attention and belief in, so do you, but now it needs to come from you to you. Only in the relationship with self can you find true independence and leave behind the dependency of childhood. Certainly, be with people who love and believe in you, but primarily rely on yourself to affirm your worth, genius and creativity. In making this resolution hold onto the words of the Russian dramatist and philosopher, Stanislavsky: 'the longest and most exciting journey is the journey inwards.'

Safety at Work

Traditionally, safety at work has focused on ensuring that the physical environment is not a threat to the physical wellbeing of employees. More recently, there have been some inroads made in creating sexual safety in the workplace. However, employers appear very reticent to include emotional and social safeties as safety-at-work issues. Employers need to understand that there are innumerable ways that employees can experience emotional hurt in the workplace. For many employees, the workplace is a series of emotional and social dangerous moments and the fallout from such lack of safety is causing immeasurable human misery and eroding any notion that Irish workplaces are attractive places to work. Currently, the Health and Safety Authority are handling 360,000 queries a year related to bullying. The source of these emotional and social threats is particularly present among the management strategies of middle management and senior management. These managers, who themselves are pressurised from the upper management people, are employing stress and intimidation as weapons to drive their workers harder, irrespective of the threat to wellbeing or to maintaining a positive work ethos. Absenteeism, sabotage, sickness and bullying claims are costing industry millions of euros every year and yet nobody seems to be waking up to the fact that harassment will never achieve higher job satisfaction or increased productivity. A discontented, frightened and hurt worker is not in a psychological state to give of his/her productive best.

Management needs to be primarily about leadership that is both of a nurturing and enabling nature. The leaders or managers of work organisations that are not wise to this essential reality need to seriously reflect and review the government style being practised. All of the safeties mentioned are part and parcel of the relationship required between managers and employees. Emotional and social safeties are created by a relationship that is person-centred and affirming and does not confuse the actions of a worker with his or her person. Irrespective of how good or poor is an employee's productivity, a respectful relationship needs to be maintained. No action on the part of an employee merits being 'put down' or 'put up' on a pedestal. Certainly, responsible, productive and creative responses need to be encouraged, praised and rewarded but not confused with the employee's person. Equally, irresponsible actions need to be firmly confronted without jeopardising the relationship.

Employees who are told 'you're great', 'wonderful', 'superior' are just as much at emotional risk as those who are ridiculed, berated, marginalised and labelled as 'useless', 'slow', 'incompetent' because of their failure to measure up. It is the mature manager that maintains a clear distinction between the person and actions of an employee. However, it would appear that such maturity is rare, as the source of harassment being experienced by employees is from middle and senior management and not from their own colleagues. Furthermore, the indications are that individuals occupying posts at these management levels are being harassed themselves by senior management. Indeed, the Irish Business and Employers' Federation (IBEC) has resisted incorporating warnings about bullying into

Leabharlanna Fhine Gall

workplace safety statements. IBEC is also objecting to those employees who have been motivated to take court action to secure their rights. However, this objection does not stop an individual employee seeking redress through the courts.

It is unlikely that any major progress in reducing the level of bullying will occur until middle and senior managers stand up for their right to respect and a positive work ethos. Of course, progress could be considerably speeded up if upper management people reflected on their own management and leadership styles and adopted an approach that enhances relationships rather than one that creates emotional and social unsafety. It is a serious indictment of our society that while we have come to some level of maturity around physical and sexual harassment, we have not even remotely begun to accept that emotional hurting is widespread and has devastating effects on people's self-esteem. What entrepreneurs and all levels of management personnel need to understand is that there is no one who comes into the workplace without emotional baggage. The ordering of human affairs cannot be achieved by any organisation where the managing of it depends on people who themselves are slaves of egoism, vanity, ambition, success, the desire for power, suspicion, distrust, partiality and prejudice. However, vulnerability, of its very nature puts pressure on others. Clearly, individuals in management positions who are insecure, fearful and dependent are not in the mature place to manage others. All the evidence is that their insecurities lead to all sorts of defensive manoeuvres that more often than not are of an aggressive and intimidating nature.

It is incumbent on leaders of work organisations to ensure that they select individuals for management positions who have a high degree of maturity. Of course, there is no guarantee that these leaders are in a place of mature consciousness to do that! When that is the case, the leaders get the managers that will mirror their own defensiveness. This organisation is seriously stuck in an immaturity warp. In situations where leaders become conscious of their unsatisfactory selection of managers, then opportunities to reflect on and progress from their defensive ways is an urgent requirement. The manager who does not take up such an opportunity cannot be allowed continue is his role. The leader of an organisation that allows this manager to continue is engaging in serious neglect of employees, of self and the organisation.

Examining Relationships

There is the surprising statistic that Ireland is the safest country in Europe to live in (United Nations 2010). In many ways the comparison of homicide and assault rates across twenty-seven European countries does not make a lot of sense, as even one killing or one assault in any country is just one too much. The finding too that with 0.32 killings per l00,000 people Ireland is the safest country is no cause for celebration. The 2005 figure of 0.32 per l00,000 people masks the dark reality that as a country we have developed a culture where violence and murder are an everyday experience. The tragic truth is that in 2005 there were sixty-five murders and manslaughters. In 2007 that figure rose to eighty-four (Central Statistics Office).

Plato, the Greek philosopher, said that 'a life unexamined is a life not worth living'. Surely it is also true to say that a culture unexamined is a culture not worth having. Something radical has changed in Irish society where parents are taking their children's (and spouses') lives and then their own or where a son takes the lives of his parents and then takes his own life. It is certainly possible to identify some of the broad strokes in modern Ireland that may account for the precious lives of others and the sacred lives of children being taken so violently. Materialism, the fall off in religious practice, social isolation, desensitisation to violence, the confusion of what, if any, values to hold, the rise of atheism and the consequent loss of belief in anything beyond what one sees are obvious examples. I have no doubt that each of these factors contributes to the present ways we live, but if change is to come about, we need to examine the situation more deeply and more closely, in particular how these sad individuals who took lives related to themselves, partner, family, children, friends, employer and fellow employees and how, in turn, all of these significant people related to them.

The deepest need of a human being is to belong. This need arises from an innermost place and its purpose is to create the safety and security for the true and unique nature of each individual to emerge. Individuals are often hurt, disappointed and devastated by an over-belonging or an under-belonging or absolutely no sense of belonging. An over-belonging is where you have to live your life for another (parent, spouse, lover, friend, employer). An under-belonging relationship is where another (parent, spouse, lover, friend, employer) should live their life for you. These two kinds of relationships prevent the emergence of the mature belonging to one's self that is critical to the wellbeing of society. When one possesses an inner stronghold you can bring a maturity, creativity, love, understanding and hope to others. What you have found in yourself you support and nurture in others.

No sense of belonging is where your existence has not mattered and a great interior darkness descends on you and your daily companions are alienation, despair, hopelessness, rage at others or at yourself.

It is not too difficult to detect these kinds of troubled relationships among people and to create the opportunities for change in the sad circumstances of these people's lives. However, the emotional and spiritual wellbeing of our people have not been a priority in our culture because it entails all of us needing to examine our inner and outer lives. Until we create the safety for individuals to own, express and seek resolution to their doubts of their unique worthiness or what they perceive as the apparent meaninglessness of life, I do not see our culture becoming more enlightened.

Dangerous to be Real

Sometimes, one of the hardest things to do is to be *real*, to be authentic, to be genuine, to speak out what you truly feel, think and need. *Being real* is never about talking about somebody else, but it is about talking and taking action for self. There are those who believe you should say straight out what you feel and think, whether it is about self or another. However, if you call your manager 'stupid' or 'histrionic' or 'a controller', you are not being real, but you are being defensive. Anytime we send a 'you' message, we are hiding what we *really* want to say. In the examples given, the authentic message could be: 'I'd like my opinion to be at least listened to' and 'I have a need to discuss issues calmly' and 'I'd prefer to make my own decisions on this issue.'

What is it that makes it difficult for us to be real? The answer is that it can be dangerous to be real – physically, sexually, emotionally, intellectually, behaviourally, socially, creatively and spiritually. The greater the threat, the more unlikely it is that you will risk speaking your truth. Children learn this defence early on when they know the risks of not conforming to the demands and expectations of a parent/teacher who dominates and controls or is passive and over-protective.

A good question to ask about a couple relationship – husband-wife, lover-lover, friend-friend, parent-adult offspring, manager-employee is: 'is this relationship a series of dangerous moments with a few safe ones?' or 'is this relationship a series of safe moments with a few dangerous ones?' Clearly, when it is the latter scenario, it is safe to be real in most situations, with maybe one or two taboo subjects. In the former relationship, most topics pose a threat and conformity would appear to be the safer option. Certainly, in the case of children, conformity is the safest option, unless they can find some adult who will champion their just cause. Adolescents frequently attempt to find support to be real from their peer group and this change of events can give rise to many emotional storms within the family. Adults cannot afford to wait for others to make the world a safe place for them to be true to themselves. However, unless you have come into a fairly solid place of acceptance of self and separateness from the threats posed by others, you are more likely to continue to conform to the ways and expectations of those whose reactions threaten your wellbeing. Such conformity makes for deeply unhappy relationships, and unless one of the parties to the relationship finds the mature inner place from which to speak their truth, the relationship will continue to deteriorate. Conflict, of its very creative nature continues to escalate in an attempt to wake up those in conflict to the unresolved issues that lie within each of them and between them.

However, when past experiences of attempting to 'talk things over' have been met by such threatening responses as verbal or physical aggression, hostile withdrawal and unrelenting silence, screaming, threatening to leave, to hurt self, to commit suicide, take to the bottle, swallow tablets, then it is wiser to say nothing. Not *saying* anything does not mean *doing* nothing. On the contrary, urgent action is required in such dangerous situations, but it needs to be of a nature that it does not escalate the danger to self.

One definite action you can take is to 'break the silence' on the untenable situation with a person with whom you feel emotionally safe and who will listen, be discreet, be non-judgemental and, on request, be able to suggest sound directions to take. Having such a support may help you to determine ways of confronting the person about your unhappiness. Possible strategies are:

- Write to the person
- Give him an audio-tape of your concerns
- Request somebody he respects to talk with him.

When there is no positive response to such overtures, stronger measures are required: actions always speak louder than words. Be sure that such actions are taken within a climate of unconditional positive regard. It is the behaviour and not the person that is the challenge. Possible actions are:

- Break the silence on the difficulties to a number of parties
- Attend counsellor for self
- Send a solicitor's letter
- Where there is intimidation or violence, report it to your medical practitioner and police, seek refuge and obtain a protection order from the District Court.

Frequently, any of the above actions may escalate the perpe-
trator's defensive responses of verbal aggression, control,
manipulation, silent treatment or violence. Such reactions are an
attempt to deter you from continuing your assertiveness. Sometimes,
compensatory responses emerge – weeping and promising all sorts
of changes – once you stay silent. However, these behaviours are
also defensive in nature. The best proof of change is sustained efforts
to respond to your unmet needs. A particularly good index of a
person's shift in consciousness is his/her agreement to attend for
either individual or relationship counselling. Refusal generally means
a short-lived experience of moving towards a mature relationship.

'CAVE' Dwellers

Typically, in the human resources literature, three kinds of
employees are identified:

- those who are highly engaged
- those who are disengaged
- those who are 'CAVE dwellers' (quotes are mine)

The reason why I put the 'CAVE dwellers' in quotes is because I
believe individuals are not their behaviour and that such judgements
serve only to perpetuate the very behaviour that is being scrutinised!
The poll done by the Gallup Oranisation, India, in 2008 (quoted in
an article: 'Of Caves and Cultures', in *The Human Factor*, October
2008) found that twenty per cent of employees are highly engaged
and that the other eighty per cent is divided between the second two
categories. 'CAVE dwellers' are described as 'constantly against virtually everything' – hence CAVE. Employers tend to invest in those
employees who are highly engaged and go to considerable lengths
in terms of promotions and financial packages to retain such staff.
There appears to be an underlying assumption that employees who
are highly engaged are more mature than those who occupy either
one of the other two categories. However, this assumption is inaccurate, particularly for those highly engaged workers who are addicted

to success, money, power or wealth. Any of these addictions will certainly motivate these employees to be highly engaged in their jobs but they will not make good managers. There are also high risks of burn-out, illness, marital and family breakdown and a resorting to substance addictions to support their over-engagement in work. When you consider that most people leave their jobs because of poor management, it is highly likely that the latter arises from the insecurities and fears of highly engaged employees. I would be curious to know what percentage of the twenty per cent of the highly engaged would view work, in the words of Khalil Gibran 'as love made visible'. The employee who loves work is in the mature place of integrating work as *one* of the important aspects of his or her life. The other essential aspects of living are one's own psycho-social wellbeing, significant relationships with partner, children, friends, educational development, spirituality and leisure and pleasure. It has not been the practice of work organisations to deter-mine the level of maturity of highly engaged employees before promoting them to higher posts of responsibility, but this is an omis-sion that eventually bites the hand that feeds it.

The high percentage of employees who are disengaged are into the defensive mechanism of avoidance or going for the average. When I put the above figures regarding employees to teachers and ask them to tell me what percentage of their second-level students are disengaged or minimally engaged, they will say 'anything up to eighty per cent'. This figure is alarming, not only because it matches the statistics of employees on application to work, but also because of the enormous loss of creativity and productivity. What is fasci-nating is why schools and workplaces are not asking the question: why do so many individuals underplay their amazing potential? I rarely come across a toddler that would be considered 'disengaged' and it appears to me that the answer lies in how adults view work and learning and the very significant influence this has on children's (and, subsequently, adults') motivation to learn and work. Children as young as six and seven complain of being all stressed out by tests, meaning that the adventure of learning that they showed pre-school is being eroded by the seriousness with which parents and teachers view school tests. Very few adults view examinations as an adventure and even fewer have held onto their sense of a limitless potential. Being disengaged from work or just putting in an average input are clever ways of offsetting further experiences of failure, criticism, judgement, humiliation and embarrassment. Emotional, social, behavioural, intellectual, physical and creative safeties and excitement are critical to the maintenance and encouragement of a love of work and learning. These safeties are expressed through mature relationships which need to lie at the heart of teaching, learning and working. Teaching and learning without such relationships are not teaching and learning at all; similarly, work without mature relationships is not work at all.

In contrast to those who disengage through avoidance or average input, the 'CAVE' dwellers cleverly offset the spotlight being shone on their minimal work efforts by constantly criticising virtually everything. By vehemently and persistently putting the blame on their colleagues, managers, the work organisation, the unions, the family, the government and the EU, these employees manage effectively to offset failure, criticism and humiliation by ensuring that their constantly being difficult means nobody will put pressure on them to improve their work attainments. The creation of the mature relationship and the various safeties outlined above are just as critical for this group of employees as for those who are passively disengaged and those who are addicted to work, success, power or wealth.

The Inner Terrain of Relationships

It is our inner terrain that totally determines how we respond to each other. It is not what another person says or does that upsets me or abhors me or uplifts me; if that were the case then I would be totally at the mercy of the 'bad' or 'good' things that I experience in a relationship with another. This is true of a lover-lover, husband-wife, parent-child, employee-manager relationship; indeed it is true of all relationships. When, for example, my boss blames me for always being late, my response will arise from whatever inner place I am at at that time. If I generally take responsibility for how another feels – a defensive strategy I have unconsciously developed – then I will respond to the blaming with feeling hurt within and totally apologetic without, bending over backwards to appease the boss's anger.

However, if I generally take responsibility for my own behaviour and believe others – including my manager – needs to take responsibility for his own behaviour, then my response to 'you're always late' will be totally different. I may now acknowledge that he is upset, apologise for being late and correct the over-generalisation of 'always' being late. I do not feel 'put down' by the manager's outburst; on the contrary, I care about him being upset, but realise that his upset is arising from his inner terrain, not from my being late. If he generally took responsibility for his own behaviour, then when it transpired that I had not arrived when expected, he would have done one of several things. When I arrived late he could have met me with his need for me to be on time with 'I have noticed you've been late several times lately and I'm wondering what's happening to cause that?' Alternatively, he could have expressed his emotional response to my being late: 'Tony, I am annoyed to see you arriving late again.' He could have left a note to say he had gone ahead with what had been planned; he could have rung me on the mobile and enquired 'what's happening?' In such scenarios he does not personalise my being late – that's my responsibility – but he does take action for himself.

Conflict between individuals arises from an inner place of insecurity, fear and dependence and the consequent need to control another to be there for you in a way that it is not safe enough for you to be there for yourself. Unless that challenge of finding an inner solidity is taken up, individuals will continually find themselves in conflict with others. The bottom line is that I am responsible for my own security, contentment and happiness and it is a recipe for unhappiness when I pass that responsibility on to others.

I recall a male associate once saying to me, 'Tony, my children are driving me wild; can you help me?' I replied, 'Sure I can help. It is not your children who are driving you wild; it is yourself. As long as you make your children responsible for your needs you will continue to have a difficult relationship with them.' I enquired, 'What are your needs in relation to the children?' He promptly answered, 'My need is for peace and quiet.' I responded, 'That's a reasonable need; so what are you doing about it?' He looked at me puzzled and said, 'It is the children that are stopping me from meeting that need.' I went on to explain that when the children meet him in the evening when he comes home from work and they want to have 'a wild time' with him that this is their need. Their need is just as legitimate as his! He can certainly make a request of the children for a period of quiet and peace, but the children may not be in a place to meet that need. When they are, great; when they are not, then the responsibility for meeting the need for peace and quiet comes back to him.

One aspect of this father's inner terrain is that he expects others to meet his needs and when they don't, he blames them and severs relationships with them – even his own children. He doesn't do that consciously, but unconsciously. The conflict draws attention to the inner vulnerability that requires conscious attention and resolution. I encouraged him to find ways of meeting his own needs, not just in his relationship with his children, but also with others – so that he at least maintains a wholesome relationship with them. In the meantime, he needed support and guidance to develop a solid interiority from which he can stay separate from the behaviour of others and not personalise those not meeting his needs as 'letting him down' or 'not loving him'. Such a solid interiority develops from an examination of our inner and outer worlds, and the creation of the relationship with self that you would like with another but is possible only with yourself.

People Care!

Following the 26 December 2004 tsunami and other human disasters, a number of writers have suggested that when we witness the suffering of others we begin to see the emptiness of the notion of self. It would appear to me that these authors have no sense of what the 'self' means and not only do they dismiss the massive psychological literature on how a person's sense of self determines how they relate to others and to the world, they also dismiss thousands of years of philosophy and spirituality that have emphasised the knowing and love of self and others. Ironically, it is the latter issue that these critics of the notion of self miss: that it is in finding regard for self that one finds love for the other and, indeed, for the world we live in. There is no suggestion that when individuals are encouraged to 'know self', to be self-independent, 'to be self' that they do not take into consideration that they live in a world where the insecurities of others and natural disasters can pose great threats to our wellbeing. The suffering of others touches us because we identify it with our own suffering. The person who does not acknowledge his own suffering is unlikely to respond to the suffering of others. This can be seen so graphically when a father who is violent towards his spouse and children denies he has any problems. Unless this father reflects on what has brought him to such numbness to the suffering of others he will not come to a place of nurturance of himself and others.

Rather than the self being a limited creation of the human mind, it is the foundation for seeing the interconnectedness between each human being. Tragedies certainly make us more aware of the interrelating that is necessary for survival. Christ was so accurate when he proclaimed 'you must love God with all your heart and your neighbour as yourself'. Psychology has shown that it is only when an individual loves self that he can truly love another. Low self-esteem (poor relationship with self) is now known to underpin depression, anxiety, marital difficulties, obsessive-compulsive difficulties, learning difficulties and most other human conflicts. Rather than the notion of self being a block to people being there for each other, particularly in times of crises, the level of a person's self-possession will determine the nature of his responsiveness to a crisis. I believe some authors confuse the need for humans 'to depend' on each other to be able to safely love, work, play and pray in this world with 'being dependent' on others for our survival. Being dependent is where I pass responsibility for my life over to others and such a 'passing of the buck' is a recipe for relationship, societal and political conflict. Certainly people need to 'inter-support' and inter-relate with each other for many cooperative responses and resources for living, but it would not be wise for people to be inter-dependent. Such dependence would leave individuals or groups open to major exploitation. Individuals who love self and are independent automatically reach out with mind and heart to the world, are the first to admit to the need for shared resources and are the champions of the oppressed. It is their independence that provides the solid ground from which they can deeply and genuinely connect with others. Such connecting with others leads to an even stronger sense of aliveness and reinforces the relationship with self.

The tsunami disaster and other tragedies have shown the enormous capacity of human beings to respond with generosity, active helping and compassion. However, deep questions need to be asked as to why some tragic events elicit such strong responses and others (that happen daily) do not. There is also the issue that kindness and compassion between all peoples are needed on a daily basis within homes, schools, communities, workplaces, churches and between countries and the pity is that it takes major crises to wake some of us up to that urgent reality.

Resolving Bullying and Passivity

The sad suicide of teenager Leanne Wolfe in late 2007 gave rise to considerable media attention on bullying and its effects on those who are targeted. The fact that bullying is a behaviour that occurs in all social systems – home, school, community, sports clubs, workplaces, churches – is not news to most people. However, what strikes me about much of the media attention is, one, no definite solutions are being put forward and, two, nobody appears to be strongly questioning why some young people who are being bullied do not communicate their difficult circumstances. Why is it that young people and, indeed, older people do not believe that people will care about what is happening to them? Furthermore, why is it that it is not being shouted from the rooftops of homes, schools, classrooms, communities, sports clubs, churches and workplaces that such threatening behaviour, whether of a physical, verbal or non-verbal nature, will not be tolerated? Is it because many of us engage in bullying ourselves and do not want to draw attention to ourselves or is it that we are passive and are not in a place to champion those, young or older, who are being bullied? And surely if this is the case, is it not important that we attempt to reduce, preferably eliminate, passivity as much as bullying?

What is often not recognised is that individuals who bully, be it child or teenager or adult, have as deep a sense of worthlessness, helplessness and hopelessness as those who are bullied. Bullying behaviour is an attempt to control another, because one has not got control over one's self. Bullying arises from fear, dependence and, ultimately, is an attempt to reduce threats to self. There is no doubt that the very nature of bullying is a serious threat to the wellbeing of another; however, it also mirrors the insecurity of the person who is bullying. There is no attempt here to dilute the threats posed by bullying or to excuse the behaviour, but unless it is understood that those who bully need as much help as those they bully, we are not likely to reduce the level of bullying in our society. Neither are we likely to reduce the level of passivity, unless we examine closely the equally threatening violence of passivity.

What lies at the heart of bullying and, indeed, passivity is how individuals interact with each other in the key social systems. Relationship, relationship, relationship is what needs ongoing examination. Those, especially, in positions of leadership – parents, school principals, teachers at all levels from pre-school to tertiary colleges, childminders, managers in workplaces, sports trainers and managers, priests, policemen, community leaders, politicians – need to daily reflect on how they relate to others. When individuals detect patterns of behaviour that are of a bullying or passive nature, then they need to urgently seek help. Others who witness bullying or passivity need to challenge these defensive responses and not rest until resolution is achieved. Turning a blind eye is not uncommon, and the responsibility for such passivity needs to be put squarely at the feet of those who engage in such violent silence. However, whereas confrontation on bullying and on passivity is essential for a progression towards mature relationships, within and between people, young and older, it is equally necessary that such confrontation be of a non-judgemental nature. Judgement, criticism, condemnation may be the very behaviours that gave rise to bullying or passivity. Understanding behaviours that reveal insecurity and are a threat to the wellbeing of others is critical to the resolution of the defensive coin that has bullying on one side and passivity on the other. It is from a place of understanding that individuals who bully or who are passive can be guided and supported towards, one, taking responsibility for the threatening nature of their actions or non-actions on others and, two, working towards the resolution of their inner turmoil and stressful relationships. Opportunities and psycho-social services need to be readily available within schools, communities and workplaces for those who need to seriously examine how they feel about themselves and how they relate to others.

The main areas that require focus to reduce bullying and passivity are:

- Support and guide those in positions of management and leadership to monitor their own responses to others and to work towards the creation of mature relationships
- For significant adults to be readily able to identify the signs and effects of bullying and passivity in homes, schools, communities and workplaces
- For adults to effectively intervene in situations where bullying and passivity are frequently present
- For adults to know how to empower at-risk children, adolescents and adults who are being bullied or are bullying
- For significant adults to be trained in how to create cultures that promotes self-esteem and assertiveness and strongly sanction, in a non-judgemental way, bullying and passive violence.

Nobody Asks to be Bullied

New research by Torunn Dahl, business psychologist at consultancy firm Pearn Kandola found that 'victims of workplace bullying are often blamed by colleagues for bringing it upon themselves' (2008 Psychological Society of Ireland Conference). Of those interviewed, up to fifty per cent blamed the victim's personality for the bullying. Typical descriptions of the person who was at the receiving end of intimidating behaviour were: 'she's trying to change things too much' or 'she's over-ambitious' or – a typical reaction – 'she's over-sensitive'. When bystanders do nothing when they witness a bullying scenario, naturally they will find ways of justifying their inaction and the blaming of the 'victim' is one such strategy.

The research also found that twenty-five per cent of those who witnessed bullying did nothing about it – some because 'they were afraid of drawing attention to themselves', others 'because they felt it was not their responsibility'. The latter response is particularly alarming. Another finding was that 'weak management was to blame for the bullying'. There is considerable truth in this response – most people leave their jobs because of 'poor' management, particularly a bullying type of management. However, this reality is not a reason for doing nothing when bullying occurs. Surely it is the responsibility of each one of us to support the dignity of each person and to take mature action when their presence is under threat from the words and actions of another. Ask yourself how you would feel if a work colleague, friend or partner stood idly by when you were being bullied?

Nobody asks to be bullied. The words and actions of an individual are always 100 per cent about that person – his or her reactions are *never* about the other person. A person who employs bullying and blames the other person – 'you drove me to shout at you' or 'your behaviour drives me wild' or 'you deserved to be hit' – is not even remotely in the ballpark of owning and taking responsibility for his or her actions. Bullying always arises from fear, but when an adult is not in a place of psycho-social readiness to examine their own fears, they will cleverly put the responsibility onto another. When this blaming occurs, it is a source of threat to the wellbeing of the targeted person. When the person targeted is also in a place of fear and low self-esteem, (s)he may not be in a place to *withstand* the defensive behaviour of the person bullying. It is in such a situation that others who are in a solid place to intervene need to do so and in a way that is decisive and non-threatening. It is crucial that the person who is being passive is not 'blamed', but opportunities for that person to become empowered need to be provided.

Equally, opportunities for resolution of fears and empowerment need to be provided for individuals who bully. What is not often appreciated is that opportunities for empowerment are also required for the bystanders and for those individuals who rationalise that those who are being bullied are asking for it. As seen above, no matter what we say and do and, in spite of ourselves, we reveal our own fears and insecurities. It is a psychological fact that everything that arises in any person – including those who are bullied, those who bully, those who stand idly by, those who blame the people at the receiving end of bullying – is about the person himself or herself. This is a hard fact to swallow, not because we don't have the intelligence to understand it, but because it involves an examination of our own interiority and can involve making difficult decisions and taking challenging actions. So when the bystanders say that 'she's trying to change things too much' or 'she's over-sensitive', owning these statements as being about oneself might mean discovering that 'change frightens me' or 'I don't like to rock the boat' or 'I'm over-sensitive to criticism and, as a result, avoid taking risks.' Of course, the source of what an individual projects onto another – for example, 'she's over-ambitious' – will have a unique source for different individuals. Projections are always opportunities for reflection but we are not always in a safe enough inner or outer space to take on that challenge. However, when such an examination of our own behaviour does not occur, the challenging and threatening situation – wherever it is arising – is likely to continue to escalate.

The Difference Between Boundaries and Defences

When conflict arises between people the more common response of the parties to the conflict is defensiveness. The inevitable result of a defensive response is an escalation of the conflict. The creative purpose of the conflict is to provide the opportunity for those in conflict with one another to examine their own interior worlds and to look at what insecurities and fears they are bringing to the relationship that is in conflict. However, the examination of our inner relationship with self is very challenging and the recourse to an attack back (attack being the best defence) or a physical or emotional withdrawal may appear the easier course to travel. Certainly, we have an inner wisdom that keeps us in a defensive place until we have found some emotional safety within and social safety without to be authentic and real.

Contrary to what many people think, a defensive reaction is not designed to hurt another. Defensive responses may be an 'acting-in' or an 'acting-out' nature or the resorting to the misuse of substances (drugs, alcohol, food) or the embodiment of the inner conflict that is being projected onto another or others. The 'acting-out' defensive response can be verbal or a physical action (such as violence, pounding an inanimate object, banging doors, etc.). The aim of these responses is to put the responsibility onto the other person so that you are protected from having to examine your own behaviour, which may mean taking some radical action that you are not yet ready to do. The 'acting-in' defensive response puts the blame on oneself – 'I'm such an awful person', 'I'm just no good'. This is a clever defence because it short circuits the other person's criticising of you, but it also effectively rules out any real examination of what it is within you that requires realisation and definitive action. Sadly, sometimes 'acting-in' can be a self-harming action, which can have the intention of 'look at what you made me do now'. 'Taking to the drink' or popping tranquilisers or anti-depressants are common defensive responses and may be saying in so many words,'I have to put myself out of it in order to live with your threats of rejection.'

However, the critical issue in the conflict with another is not about how I live with you but about how I can live with myself. Conflict arises from what each individual brings to the relationship with another in terms of their own interiority. It is the meeting between the interior worlds of individuals that gives rise to conflict, not the relationship between them. As long as each person defensively believes that it is the relationship that is the problem, little or no change will occur. Furthermore, it is only change *within* the individuals that effects enduring change *between* them.

An embodied defensive response is the unconscious employment of an illness in response to a conflict situation. Fainting during a row is not unusual and it is a very powerful defensive response. The effect is that all the attention goes on reviving the person who has fainted and the conflict issues get forgotten – until the next time.

It is only possible to resolve conflict when individuals resort to boundaries rather than defences. A boundary calls for an action *for self*, whereas a defence leads to either an action *against* another or oneself. A boundary is the visible or invisible line you draw around your own worth and dignity as a unique human being. It is that *strong hold* of self in the face of any threats to your wellbeing; it is holding to an inner solidity from which nobody has the power to demean, lessen or dismiss your presence. It is a *proactive* rather than a *reactive* place; it is a place of confident responsibility – for self and for one's own actions. It is an active assertiveness of your own worth, value, dignity, individuality and sacredness. When conflict arises, the person who is in that conscious self-reliant place will resort to boundaries and take definite action for self in a way that does not threaten the wellbeing of another. Easier said than done, but it is only through continual work on our inner self that such maturity is possible. An example of a boundary in response to somebody 'rubbishing your beliefs or values' would be: 'I'm interested to know what reasons have you for aggressively dismissing my beliefs.' This response means that the person holds his or her own dignity, is open to discussion and has provided the other person with the opportunity to examine his or her own defensive response. Of course, there is no guarantee that the person will take up that opportunity, but as long as one person stays in a solid place of boundary, the conflict will not escalate and responsibility will be left with the person who remains defensive to examine his or her own reactions: the person who proacts is already in that self-responsibility place.

Feedback and Wellbeing

One of the dreaded experiences of many employees is performance appraisal, an annual audit of their work performance. It is interesting that work organisations persist with this mechanism even though it is a dreaded experience. It is similar to a teacher or lecturer persisting with a teaching method that students hate.

Employees find performance appraisals threatening because, one, the appraisals are judgemental and, two, are a one-way street. Certainly, employees are encouraged to state their own case about their work, but the final rating is done by the manager or director. There is no space for the employee to do a similar appraisal on the manager. This is a deficit I have long questioned – who evaluates the top managers? To suggest that they evaluate themselves would not be wise, because their position is absolutely no guarantee of personal maturity. For performance appraisals to be fair and just there needs to be a level two-way playing field.

There is a more serious issue to be considered and that is that, by their very nature, performance appraisals are seen as threatening and more often than not generate anxiety. Indeed, the most common anxiety in schools and workplaces is performance anxiety. A more effective way of considering an employee's work progress is to provide an opportunity for *mutual feedback* between the employee and the manager who is representing the work organisation. Similarly, in classrooms and lecture rooms, students need to be able to provide feedback of their experiences at the hands of teachers and the school system. One of the underlying causes for our present economic crisis is that those at the top of financial organisations were not accountable to anybody. All work, educational and other social systems require an inbuilt means of accountability for each member, particularly those who hold most responsibility.

The word feedback symbolically means to nurture, and an employee's own feedback on his year's work needs to be an exercise in determining what has been achieved and what new challenges arise from past and present endeavours – whether these are low, average or high. Progress can only be built on what is present; it rarely emerges from a performance appraisal that emphasises deficits in performance. Feedback is to attempt to deepen wellbeing and progress for the individual employee and the work organisation. Similarly, when an employee provides feedback on his experiences of management and the organisation's culture, the aim needs to be to nurture what is mature. Feedback throws light on the organisation's growth that has been developed to this point in time and provides the basis for enhancement of that growth.

A vital aspect of feedback is that it is always about the person providing it. When a manager gives feedback to an employee, it is important that he realises that what he is saying is about himself – his expectations, his needs and goals. No one can evaluate the work of another; what they can do is report *their responses* to the employee's endeavours, but they need to make sure that they *own* these responses as being about themselves. Similarly, when an employee provides feedback on the manager's practices and the structures and work procedures of the organisation, it shows a maturity to view that feedback as being about the employee and the degree to which his needs, expectations and work goals have been met by the manager and the work organisation. No progress can be made when the feedback given is seen as being about the person or system being considered and not the person providing the feedback. Regrettably, performance appraisals are not viewed with such clarity and maturity.

Psycho-social wellbeing of employee, irrespective of the level of responsibility held, is a key issue within a work organisation. It is about people before profits; it is also about emotional and social prosperity being coupled with economic prosperity. Annual or bi-annual feedback opportunities for *all* members of the organisation is one way of checking up on how well the organisation and management is meeting its responsibilities towards employees; it is also an opportunity to examine the degree of personal accountability of *each* employee, especially those individuals who hold top positions.

Facing Up to Facial Expression

Let's face it, the face says it all! But does it? After all, the face is as good at masking emotions as it is at expressing them. In both of these ways, facial expression serve powerful functions – one, to suppress what arises in us and, two, to express the emotions present. Certainly, it is far more threatening to your mature progress and wellbeing to hide your inner turmoil so that nobody but nobody gets a look in to your interiority. However, we mask those feelings that are too threatening to reveal and we learn that lesson very early on in life. So many adults I have worked with relate stories of, as children, having to have a happy facial expression and daring not to show such emergency feelings as upset, anger, fear, disappointment and hurt. They unconsciously realised the dangers of emergency emotional expression, namely that a parent or a significant adult would not be able to cope with distress. Children, in their wisdom, create the defensive response to such a threat and put on the happy face to offset the threat. To paraphrase the poet Elliot, they 'put on the face to meet the face'. Infants and children are far more expert than adults at reading faces – and for good reasons. They often carry their defensive masks into adulthood and some crisis – physical, emotional, social, occupational – may need to occur before they come into conscious realisation that they allow nobody to get to know them. The daunting tasks are to make new choices to be authentic, real, spontaneous and open with others and to let go of the need to protect others, particularly parents and authority figures, from encountering distress. Individuals have told me that 'my mother will fall apart if I tell her how I really feel' or 'my father won't be able to cope with my telling him about my depression' or the boss would explode if *I express what I really feel about his management style*. However, if the truth be told, it is the person themselves, now as adults, who is afraid of 'falling apart' for they, like their parent or manager, have not learned to accept and resolve distress. When nobody takes responsibility within such families and workplaces, then no change occurs and the unresolved emotional repression passes from generation to generation. Be assured that we all have immense power to resolve emotional and other distresses, but not too many people are told that.

If it is important for the person who smiles all the time to become conscious of their typical facial expression, it is equally crucial for those who wear their hearts, not only on their sleeves, but on their face, to own what belongs to them and not put responsibility onto others for resolution of their inner issues, or, indeed, for their overall wellbeing. If tone of voice can pose threats to the wellbeing of others so too can facial expression. As we have seen, children need to put on the defensive face to meet the defensive face of the adults who are responsible for their care; however, adults need to get to know themselves, establish independence in relationships and take complete responsibility for their own mature progress. 'The face that stops the clock' is worn by the person who has not yet faced up to being truly adult.

One of the perplexities about reading facial expressions is that it involves so many bodily organs – the eyes, the eyebrows, the forehead, the eyelids, the cheeks, the jaw, the nose, the lips and the teeth. So, for example, we experience 'the eyes as being the windows of the soul', 'the raised eyebrow', 'the furrowed brow', 'the rapid eye-blink', 'the sucked-in cheeks', 'the jaw set against the world, 'the lips sealed', 'the nose in the air' and 'the teeth bared'. Putting the various signals together we can experience the overall facial expression as dark, startled, shocked, hard, soft, guarded, relaxed and surprised, and so on. However, we tend to interpret facial expression more in emotional terms such as hostile, appeasing, terrifying, angry, tense, sad, jealous, cheerful, mischievous, depressed, anxious, closed, open and threatening. Whatever way we interpret another person's facial expression, it is expedient that we own our interpretation as being about ourselves and not put the responsibility onto the other person. In any case, a person who shows a defensive face is not in a place to take responsibility for self, not to mind anybody else! It is the mature response to look to what action we need to take to ensure that our wellbeing is not jeopardised by what belongs to another; we can only hope that they will face their own inner demons.

Asking For What You Want

I have long contended that each of us is responsible for self and for our own needs; if that is true you might ask, 'what need do we have of other relationships?' Many of our adult needs are met in relationship with others – friends, partners, work colleagues, teachers, lecturers, managers, service providers, politicians and so on. However, having a need of another does not mean I am dependent on him or her to meet that need; on the contrary, it is my need and I am responsible for it. When I am independent I have no resistance to expressing a need but it is a request, not a demand or a command. However, when I am dependent, the expression of a need is implicitly and, often, explicitly, a demand or command. To say 'no' means risking either a verbal onslaught or an emotional and physical withdrawal that may last for days on end – until the 'offending' party breaks the ice. Sadly, sometimes, the reaction can last for years or never be resolved. There are some individuals who defensively do not express their needs, but who do expect you to read their minds – thereby cleverly putting all the responsibility onto you for not only meeting their needs but also identifying them – an impossible task but, nonetheless, taken on by some individuals. It is very empowering to identify, own and take responsibility for our own needs; it is a recipe for conflict not to do so. Because of the frequent lean-to nature of our first relationships with each parent, 'passing the buck' is very common. Of course, for every person who 'passes the buck' there is somebody who 'takes it' and protectively burdens herself with responsibility for the other person's needs. In order for change to come about, a raising of consciousness is required that either says, 'I am not responsible for another adult's needs' or 'the other person is not responsible for my needs'. Such a realisation helps the process of cutting the ties that bind. Certainly, in my own case, I would have unconsciously believed that the way to get recognition within the family was to 'look after everybody'. There is a great wisdom in that strategy because children need some sense of belonging where unconditional belonging is not present. Other adults, when children, develop the opposite strategy; they find ways to make sure that they are looked after by others – through temper tantrums, histrionics, destructiveness, aggression, violence. All of these latter behaviours are designed to ensure conditional recognition. However, whatever happened to us as children, only we can resolve as adults. Therefore, when we find ourselves engaging in demanding or commanding or waiting for others to mind-read or always attending to others, it is time to reverse the process so that responsibility for one's own needs rests with self and not with the other and that:

- demands/commands become requests
- waiting to be mind-read becomes an honest expression of a need
- attending to others becomes allowing others to speak and take responsibility for themselves.

Making the above u-turns is not easy but it is an essential part of becoming mature. It is such a place of freedom when you start taking responsibility for your own life and allow others to take responsibility for themselves.

In terms of the parenting and teaching of children, guiding children in age-appropriate ways towards responsibility for their own needs is a fundamental aspect of mature parenting. Of course, children need to be encouraged to make requests, but we have all encountered children who will scream the house down to get their own way or will sulk, withdraw or even get sick to get a need met.

Somehow, these children are not encountering the boundaries that need to be created by parents that say 'sometimes I can meet your need and sometimes I cannot, but ultimately your need is yours'. It is important to keep in mind that these children may be future managers and leaders!

In adult relationships, some individuals are scared of taking the risk to express separateness and independence for fear of the other person's reaction. When this is the case there is a deeper issue that needs resolution – non-possession of your self. When you realise that nobody owns anybody, and that individuals need to belong to their own interiority, you are then ready to take responsibility for your own needs and not take responsibility for another's needs.

6 Genius of Consciousness

The Genius of Consciousness

As part of the preparation for this collection of essays I examined the literature on training for managers and discovered an emphasis on proscriptions, coaching, employee engagement, talent mentoring and e-learning. What was glaringly absent in my search was the fact that we have an *unconscious* and also that leaders and managers, like the rest of us, carry considerable emotional baggage into their roles, which, inevitably, interrupts their effectiveness. Another missing link was a focus on *affectiveness* and the reality that mature governorship is both a head and heart phenomenon. We have seen in all the economic, political, social and health service crises besetting us here in Ireland and some other western countries that is was predominantly men who occupied positions of power, and, sadly, with devastating results. Notoriously, men operate from a 'head' space and ignore, dismiss or ridicule a 'heart' space. But good leadership and management need to *affect* (influence) employees and customers in order to *effect* (*bring about*) progressive results. Indeed, being affective and effective are inseparable partners when it comes to mature management – wherever we live, learn, pray, work and play. If the men on top had been operating from heart places then the greed, narcissism, avarice, depersonalisation of employees and customers, bullying, arrogance, superiority, corruption and cover-ups that are now so evident would not have happened. However, even though accountability, responsibility and authenticity need to be forthcoming from those leaders and managers, compassion is also required. Witch-hunts and blaming only serve to push them further into hiding. I do believe that those in power operated *unconsciously*

– were driven by hidden fears, insecurities, addictions to success, power, 'being right' and wealth. Unconsciously, there had to be present within them the goodness of their nature, hungry and thirsty for love and recognition. When the latter is the case, substitutes are unconsciously sought, and this process would have begun in their childhood years in their homes, classrooms and community.

When any individual is mis-taken by his parent or teacher or significant person for academic achievements, for success, for 'being the best', for 'being a star', for 'being good' or ridiculed for 'being bold', for 'failure', for 'making a mess', then a darkness descends on the person and the drive to maintain the token recognition becomes overwhelming. These children ingeniously conform to the unrealistic expectations or the 'put down' labels, leading to the mistaking of their precious worth and presence with what they do. They creatively devise powerful ways of staying on the pedestal or keeping their heads below the parapet. All their intelligence and creativity go into sanctifying the mistake and, repeatedly, this sanctification is often reinforced by teachers, lecturers and employers. What is even sadder is that when these men marry they will unwittingly repeat the mistake with their own children and when they are in positions of power they repeat it with employees and customers, and woe betide those who rebel. Incidentally, it was the 'highly engaged' managers and leaders who collected the huge monetary bonuses and misspent public monies. What is emerging now is that these rewards were a redundant exercise and only added to the mess we are experiencing. In any case, work is intrinsic to our nature; to over-extrinsically reward work destroys the true nature of work – this is true of learning as well.

The absence of any reference to the unconscious in the management training literature makes defensive sense, because who in a work (or other) organisation is in a consciously mature and solid place to challenge immature management? One of the most common phenomena at staff meetings is silence – passivity, often of a passive-aggressive nature – where what needs to be challenged goes unchallenged, where what needs to be brought to consciousness, stays in the unconscious. Whether you occupy the lower, middle or higher echelons of power and you turn a blind eye to what is threatening to people's emotional, social, spiritual and economic wellbeing and, ultimately, an organisation's progress, you require as much help as those who are perpetrating the neglect.

How then can organisations create the emotional and social safety for 'highly engaged' managers to allow to come to consciousness what has lain hidden for decades? No change is possible without such consciousness – consciousness of fears, insecurities and confused identities, i.e. the mistakes. A determined effort is required to create the relationship environment that will lead to an increase in managers' consciousness, so that the genius they have employed unconsciously in developing and reinforcing their defensive strategies can be unleashed into their consciousness for the good of all, mostly themselves. Some of these individuals who occupy top political, religious, corporate and educational positions and who are deeply defensively entrenched require one-to-one psychodynamic help.

The conscious manager operates from the fullness and goodness of his awesome nature and creates a work environment where it is a joy to come to work; neither will he stand idly by when dark and defensive practices are present – oh if it were only so!

The Truth Will Set You Free

It seems synchronistic that when the Olympic Games were being hosted in China, Yiyun Li, the young Chinese author, was here in Ireland to read at the Kilkenny Arts Festival. Yiyun Li won the inaugural Frank O'Connor Short Story Award as well as many other literary awards. At a time when truth is what is urgently required in international politics, her survival of a Chinese regime where people were and are depersonalised and dare not speak the truth is a testament to the unconquerability of the human spirit.

What happens in politics begins within the dynamics of the home. Individuals are not born tyrants; their early traumatic experiences determine the survival strategies they create, some of which can be absolutely terrifying in nature. When as adults these traumatised individuals are in positions of power – political, social, religious, educational and familial – their defensive behaviours are a great threat to the wellbeing of their charges. A vicious cycle ensues, because those individuals who are now under threat have no alternative but to resort to counter-defences, which result in an ever increasing spiral of turmoil and conflict. In working with individuals and groups who live in such threatening environments I can often trace the origins of the oppression back five, six or seven generations. Unless someone across those generation lines – parent, teacher, bishop, political leader, manager – examines his or her defensive ways of being, the oppression will continue. It is for this reason that those people who head familial, social, educational, religious, work and political systems have an urgent responsibility to reflect on how they are within themselves and how they are with others. When they find themselves deeply stuck in their defensive ways they need to seek help outside of themselves to break the defensive deadlock. Only the expression of truth can break this vicious cycle and it is both an individual and collective responsibility that we strive to break the silence on oppression and declare the truth of the sacredness of each human being. Christ said that 'the truth will set you free'. How right he was, but the reality is that speaking the truth, being real and authentic are the most challenging responsibilities of all, not because we do not want to but because the consequences can be hugely emotionally and socially threatening, even life-threatening.

In the face of oppression, many of us learned the defensive strategies of 'keeping mum', 'swallowing our feelings and grievances', 'turning a blind eye to neglect', 'keeping silent in the face of neglect', 'hiding the truth' and 'leaving truth that needed to be spoken unsaid'. Many of us were raised in families where the unspoken rule was 'don't upset your mother' or 'don't upset your father.' Our experiences in schools were that it is cheeky to speak the truth and that 'the teacher knows best'. In churches you dare not question dogma and in countries you dare not 'cry freedom'. The oppression of truth is on a continuum but there are few individuals who feel safe enough to be truthful in all situations.

Yiyun Li's mother became paranoid during the Maoist regime and this defensive creation escalated following the massacre in Tiananmen Square where truth was brutally crushed. Paranoia is a wise madness because it knows the terrifying consequences of speaking the truth. One of the most common illusions we create is that we all came from happy families. The other illusion, probably less common now, is that 'schooldays were the best days of our lives'. Gandhi spoke wisely about what he called 'the seven deadly sins': 'pleasure without conscience', 'knowledge without character', 'wealth without work', 'science without humanity', 'politics without principle', 'commerce without humanity' and 'worship without sacrifice'. In many ways all of these 'sins' can be put under the one 'sin' – 'relationship without truth' – which is the greatest threat to the survival of humanity.

Unless the truth is spoken within familial, social, work, educational, religious and political systems, no progress can be made in reducing man's inhumanity to man. Until people are put before profits, dignity before pleasure, truth before knowledge, people before science, humanity before commerce and truth before politics, the creative ways individuals and groups have developed to hide the truth will continue and human suffering will endure.

What Arises in Me is About Me

An unspoken secret is that 'what arises in me is about me' and any attempt to voice that truth can be responded to with considerable hostility. Of course, such hostility is a revelation of the inner world of the person who is being aggressive, a reality that could be dangerous to voice for the person being authentic.

What is it that makes it so difficult to own what arises in me as being about me – be it a dream, feeling, thought, image, action, word, non-verbal response or illness? The answer to that question lies in the answer to another question: has my life to date been a series of empowering moments with few threatening ones or a series of threatening moments with few empowering ones? If the former was the case, it is more likely you are in a place where you own what arises in you as being about you. However, if your experience was the latter one, then owning and being responsible for what arises in and from you could prove highly threatening.

When I *own* what arises in me, I will speak and act from an 'I' place, a place of responsibility and self-realisation. When I disown what arises I tend to speak from a 'you' or 'they' place and blame another, the system, the world, even God for how my life is. There is a great wisdom – though not a maturity – in such projections. The wisdom is that I shine the spotlight of blame and responsibility onto others, thereby cleverly exonerating myself from being criticised and judged. Resolution of these projections can only be brought about by the person finding the help and support to hold and value every-thing that arises as being about self. In this present economic recession, unless political and financial leaders accept responsibility for their disastrous financial, emotional and social practices, it is unlikely that anything will be learned from the present crisis. Experi-ence has shown us time after time that we do not learn from history. To own our mistakes, our fears, our vulnerabilities, our aggression, greed, avarice, rigidities . . . appears to be a bridge too far for many individuals. However, it is a bridge that each of us needs to cross. It is in each person taking responsibility to understand themselves that real progress can be made within society. It is individuals who make decisions – not systems – and it is only individuals that can choose to make different decisions. In this way, it becomes possible for each of us to affect the world at large by bringing an authenticity to the people we interact with and the social, work and spiritual systems we live in. All very well to say, but a major challenge to take on. How can this mature process be encouraged and supported?

The future of society never lies with children – it is always with adults. It is adults who need to find the safety and support to reflect on how each relates to self, to others and to the world. Whether we like it or not, we continually spill the beans on our interior world with every thought, word, feeling and action. When we begin the process of holding each manifestation of our interiority and examine what it is revealing about the relationship with self and what new choices and actions are being called, then progress towards maturity, self-realisation and taking responsibility for self and our own words and actions is taking place. Such reflection and contemplation will result in radically different ways in how we are in this world, a radicalism that is direly needed in the world today.

It is not optional for me to own what arises in me as being about me – it is a core responsibility. It is critical that leaders – in particular parents, teachers, politicians, bankers, psychologists, social workers, managers, scientists, doctors, psychiatrists – take up the challenge of knowing self so that they can create the emotional, social and intellectual safety for others to retain the authentic expression that they so powerfully and eagerly start out with.

Is it Me, You or We?

When a partner says to you 'You never listen to me', is she talking about her relationship with you or is she unconsciously talking about her self-relationship. It appears to me this is an important question and will determine not only what action is needed (or not needed) on either the part of the giver or the receiver of the message but also on the progress of the relationship between the couple. Even more crucially, the answer to the question can have critical consequences on the progress of each party's conscious self-reliance.

If the receiver hears the message as a judgement and a criticism, he is likely to respond defensively and the resultant 'heat of the conflict' will only add to the unhappy situation. Little exploration is needed to show that this personalising by the receiver is not the desirable route to go. Individuals seem more ready to recognise that the statement 'you never listen to me' is about the person making it and the wise thing to do is to return what has been said to the sender, for example 'What has brought you to say that?' The likelihood is that you may get a quick retort: 'Because you never listen.' Now it can sometimes be the case that your partner 'never listens' but it is important not to confuse his issue with your issue 'to be listened to'. The question you need to ask yourself is 'why do I put up with such non-listening?' Is it because there is a deeper non-listening going on within myself? Surely if I was in a safe and secure place to consciously hold and express my wholeness, I would have communicated a very definite message from my core self to my partner that 'I listen to myself and when not listened to by you, I will assert my position and take due action for myself if it continues.'

It seems to me that when the statement 'you never listen to me' is examined within the context of the self-relationship; all the responsibility lies with the sender of the message. Certainly, the sender can send a clear message about self and say, 'I'm requesting to be listened to when I speak.' However, a request is not a demand or a command – these put the responsibility for action on the unmet need onto another. A request is an expression of what I do for myself and what I would like from another. When the other person is not in a place to respond to my request, I do not judge, complain, criticise or gossip about her. I know that her non-listening is an unconscious revelation of an aspect of her self-relationship and I feel compassion for my partner's plight. However, compassion does not mean abandonment of self and, if following mature invitations to discuss the untenable situation the person is not ready to address the situation, then I will follow through on the listening to myself and take action for myself on the upholding of my dignity.

Given the above, it would appear that our responses to others are *not* about our relationships with them but on aspects of the inner self-relationship that is requiring conscious examination. As long as I believe that my responses are about my relationship with another, my focus stays *outside* of myself and the inner path of conscious self-reliance is not travelled.

A good question to pose is: if my responses to another's behaviour are about my own inner relationship, what then is a relationship with another all about? In my opinion, a relationship with another is where each appoints the other the guardian of their solitude and of their ability to take responsibility for self. Such responsiveness shows belief in the other and supports their taking responsibility for self. In this environment of mutual support of each partner's potential to be self-reliant, expressed needs are much more likely to be responded to. The key issue is that such mature responsiveness does not entail taking responsibility for another but is a genuine choice on the part of the receiver of the request. Authenticity would mean being ready to be able to say 'no' to a request, but communicating the 'no' in a way that mirrors the inner world of the responder: for example, 'Right now I'm not in a place to listen to what you are saying as I need to first look after some unmet needs of my own.' When the person who initially made the request hears the 'no' as being about her partner's inner self-relationship, she can acknowledge where he is at and repeat her request at another time. Both sender and receiver can now hold their relationship with one another and return comfortably and without threat to their own self-relationship. There are great grounds for feeling optimistic about the mature progress of this relationship.

The above reality can be practised in all other couple relationships – parent and child, friend and friend, teacher and pupil, employer and employee, manager and staff member, doctor and client and so on. It is a reality I return to many times because of the over-prevalence of lean-to-relationships and the under-prevalence of relationships where each person consciously takes responsibility for self and supports that maturity in each other.

Being Affective in your Profession

Being *effective* is the ambition of those of us in educational, health and industrial professions. However, what is often not appreciated, by men in particular, is that being *affective* is an essential aspect of being effective. The mind without affect is not mind at all. Equally, the practice of a profession is not practice at all without heart. The word 'affect' means to influence and the word 'effect' means to cause, to get a result. It appears to me that these two words are inextricably linked; they are bedfellows that when used together have the potential to bring about powerful and enduring change.

A professional approach that is not affective in nature in that it does not encompass concern for each individual manager and employee, or teacher and student, or health professional and client can act like a dark force in the lives of those exposed to it. Men have typically referred to *affective* qualities as the 'soft' aspect of management, but is it not ironic how 'hard' it is for men to embrace an affective approach in their professional lives. There is no mystery to this reality, as males are channelled into believing that it is a weakness to show emotion. The opposite is the case – it is a profound weakness (in the 'defensive' meaning of that word) not to be affective! The irony of it all is that when professionals lead with both head and heart they themselves are far more balanced and effective and they create an environment where a sense of belonging is felt by their charges.

Where does the fear of being affective begin? The reality is that the ability to perceive and express an affective experience is a fairly recent phenomenon. There are still cultures in the world today that do not value and often punish the perception and expression of emotions. In many workplaces such a taboo exists, as it does in many schools and health services. Within families – and each family is a unique sub-cultural group – there can be a ban on emotional expression, more so for male children. Children frequently get the messages 'don't feel what you are feeling', 'don't feel too deeply', 'don't be so intense', 'feelings are dangerous', 'feelings can lead to you being out of control', 'you are weak when you show feelings'. The reality is that feelings don't disappear because we are told not to have them. Feelings creatively arise; they are there to give expression to needs or the reality of unmet needs. When children or adults repress or suppress their feelings in a creative and protective response to the dangers of emotional expression, these buried feelings will find substitute means of expression – substance addictions or illness or emotional outbursts that appear to happen 'out of the blue'.

In terms of the wellbeing of children and their roles as future professionals, it is critical that the adults responsible for their care and education allow children to express their honest feelings and say in words or vibrationally 'I am so pleased you are letting me know how you are feeling'. The most powerful way to encourage and support children to be emotionally expressive is for the adults to model emotional authenticity; this means expressing openly how they are feeling in ways that they take responsibility for themselves and for their own feelings, thoughts and actions. Children necessarily take their cues from adults and it is crucial that the significant adult males and females in *all* children's lives model emotional expression and receptivity.

Emotional *expression* is about revealing feelings as they arise with the realisation that these are about the person experiencing them, and adults need to help children to own their feelings and to communicate the unmet needs that give rise to the emotions. On the other hand, emotional *receptivity* is about the other person being open to listening to another's emotional expression and holding to the realisation that what is being emotionally expressed is not about them but the person who is either expressing a welfare or an emergency feeling.

It has not been the practice for managers of social systems to 'know themselves' before embarking on their managerial or leadership responsibilities. To 'know self' is to appreciate that every feeling, thought, image, dream and action that arises in us is about us and calling for us to take responsibility for self. If this is true for us, it is also true for everybody else. Those in governorship roles neglect their members when opportunities are not provided on an ongoing basis for individual managers and their charges to 'know self' in the ways described. It is not a simple process because we live in a society that has fostered co-dependency rather than in-dependency. The benefits of self-reliance for systems and their members are huge. When opportunities for the development of self-reliance are not provided, systems experience great losses and their members can often have a life of misery.

Unconditional Love is the *Sine Qua Non* of Conflict Resolution

Where there is conditional relating (where you're seen for what you do) there is conflict; where there is unconditional relating (being loved for self) conflict does not arise. Unconditionality is not a licence for you or another to do what he or she likes; on the contrary, unconditional relating puts the responsibility for self and one's own actions fairly and squarely on the shoulders of each party to a relationship. Unconditionality is that place of 'I-ness', that place of separateness, that solid interiority where nothing is buried under the carpet or where everybody else is not held accountable for how you feel; they are accountable for their own actions, just as you are. On the other hand, conditionality brings about quite the opposite scenario to unconditionality. Conditionality is a defensive means of passing the buck of responsibility for your life onto another; it is the place of 'You-ness', where communication is always about the other person and there is not a consciousness present that each adult is responsible for self and for everything that arises from self. Conditionality, too, is that place of enmeshment, of entanglement, where individuals inhabit each other's space rather than occupying their own unique interiority. It is also that place of dependence, of lean-to relationship and it is the most common way that individuals relate to each other. When couple relationships are of a conditional nature, it is because it is fearful for each individual to be separate, to be independent, to be one's own self, to reside in one's own individuality, to be different, to be private and to enjoy one's own company. It is not that individuals do not know that conditionality is an entrapment; it is that it is highly dangerous to be separate. When enmeshment is extreme, murder, violence, self-harming, attempted suicide and suicide are often the consequences when one person attempts to step outside the conditions. Typical conditions are:

- 'You should be there for me'
- 'You should take responsibility for me'
- 'You should always agree with me'

- 'You should be the same as me'
- 'You should only consider my needs'
- 'You should be successful'
- 'You should conform to my ways'
- 'We should do everything together'
- 'You should let me live my life for you'
- 'You should live your life for me'.

Conditions, though always protective in nature, are tyrannical. It is a case of what I call the tyranny of the 'shoulds', 'the musts', the 'ought tos' or the 'should nots' and it is highly perilous to assert: 'I'm here to live my life and I would wish for you to take responsibility for your own life.'

Examples of the conditional 'nots' (best heard as 'knots') are:

- 'You should not have your own friends'
- 'You must not have a different opinion to mine'
- 'You must not leave me'
- 'You must not fail'
- 'You must not let me down'
- 'You ought not to have preferences of your own'
- 'You should never be late'

Conditions operate in most couple relationships and in all the different settings in which those relationships take place. The power of conditionality is that it transfers responsibility over to another and, thereby, eliminates risks of failure, judgement, criticism and rejection. Where there is conditionality between two individuals – husband-wife, manager-employee, employee-employee, parent-child, politician-citizen, teacher-student, policeman-citizen – one of the parties will employ bullying and the other passivity to maintain the conditional and enmeshed nature of the relationship. Given all of this, it is not one bit surprising that there is an unspoken secret that 'unconditionality is the *sine qua non* of conflict resolution'. As long as conditionality reigns, each person's progress is massively blocked, but unless it becomes psycho-socially safe to be real, authentic, to inhabit one's own individuality, then individuals will continue to hide behind the defensive walls of conditionality. If unconditionality was present, homes, workplaces, schools and churches would be radically different. An essential responsibility is for each adult to seek that independent, separate and alone place – the benefits for all are life-enhancing. However, as long as we seek refuge in others rather than within ourselves, the secret of unconditionality will remain unspoken.

Trusting Times

Trust is the *sine qua non* of a mature relationship, be it between a parent and a child, husband and wife, lover and lover, friend and friend, citizen and politician, client and banker, employee and manager, church-goer and priest, teacher and student. Certainly, at the moment, there has been a great betrayal of trust within government, church, banks, other financial institutions, health boards and many workplaces. It is going to take considerable personal reflection and mature action on the part of individual politicians, clergy, bankers, financiers, managers, healthcare personnel and employers to regain the trust of their clients. What is often not appreciated is that the betrayal of trust that has been part and parcel of the economic recession belies a deeper betrayal of one's own integrity. Unless the inner betrayal is resolved, the betrayal of others is highly likely to continue.

The source of the inner letting down of self can be traced back to one's earlier years and the key relationship between each parent and the child. An infant emerges from the womb fully confident of being loved and cared for and does all in its power to attract the parent to his or her unique and individual presence. When the child experiences unconditional holding for his presence and expressions of that presence – physical, sexual, emotional, intellectual, behavioural, social, creative and spiritual – he becomes secure and trusts that it is safe for him to fully reveal and inhabit his own individuality; the consequences are that he learns to trust self and significant others. This experience will be repeated with other significant people in neighbourhood, playschool, primary school and church, and so on. However, when a child experiences a lack of unconditional love, or a conditional relating or no sense of belonging, then the darkness of this betrayal leads to the powerful protective response of repression of his true self and the creation of a false/shadow self. It is in the fashioning of this false persona, this substitute presence, that the child learns to not trust his own power to be real and authentic. If the child were to show trust in self in the face of betrayal of trust by the significant others (mother, father, teachers, aunts, uncles, doctors, nurses) in his life, he would be in even greater peril! It is in this way that an inner and outer world of untrustworthiness is formed. The more betrayal of trust that occurs, the greater the inner protective betrayal has to be.

As adults, we need to examine the whole issue of trust and to determine if we are continuing to depend on others for our security rather than learning to depend on ourselves. In redeeming our trust in our own unique nature we will encounter considerable risks – the enemies are still out there – but while there is a comfort in being hidden, it is an utter calamity for ourselves and, indeed, for all others – especially significant others – when we do not find and express the fullness, breadth and depth of our individuality.

Such an inner examination needs to be integral to the training and preparation of all professionals, especially because they occupy positions of power over others and because their own unresolved inner betrayal of self can perpetrate havoc in their personal, interpersonal and professional lives. It is in this way that personal effectiveness lies at the heart of professional effectiveness and that an inner trustworthiness determines an integrity and trustworthiness in personal, interpersonal and professional relationships.

It is a very worrying situation that those professionals who betrayed the trust that clients and employees had in their care are not even remotely examining their actions. There is a frenetic scramble going on to get things back to the way they were and no consciousness that this return to defensive ways, down the road, will only lead to another recession. The word 'recession' is better understood as 'take a break' to review how the present economic crisis has come about and to examine the inner dark 'recesses' of the mind that led to the grossly neglectful actions that are apparent to many of us but not to those who perpetrated them. Lessons from history are not learned when individuals do not examine their greed, avarice, arrogance, denial, egocentricity, depersonalisation and target-fixated mentality. The only hope is that clients and voters will put a lot more trust in themselves and monitor closely the actions of those professionals to whom they entrust their health, wealth and overall wellbeing. It is best never to entrust yourself totally to anybody – professional or otherwise. Trust and take responsibility for your self and keep a keen weather eye on the professional practice of employers, managers, service providers and those who govern.

The Governorship of Self

There are two main kinds of uncertainty – internal and external. Many external kinds of political, economic, social, educational and occupational uncertainties arise from internal uncertainties. The greed, arrogance, superiority and emotional and social neglect that individuals at the top of financial and some multinational companies exhibit arise from inner insecurities. An illusion that many of us unconsciously create is that financial prosperity will lead to emotional and social prosperity. It is more realistic to say that the making of profits needs to include equal efforts to foster emotional and social security.

Profits before people have not worked and will never work. People before profits is not a common practice but, ironically, when employees are individualised and responded to in dignifying ways, they are more motivated and, as a result, responsibility, creativity and productivity rise. Many work organisations complain about employees' poor level of work engagement but do not reflect on the poor level of relationship engagement with the said employees. Frequently, organisations assume that the twenty per cent of those highly engaged in work are more mature, but often these individuals are driven by inner uncertainties and success and achievements are their way of attempting to reduce their inner insecurities. These individuals do not make effective managers or leaders, a reality that is all so clear in the present crisis in the economy, particularly the financial sector. Trust has been lost, but the trust that was there was pseudo. It is only when individuals trust themselves that they can reliably meet the entrustment that clients and employees have in them. All professions – parenting, teaching, financial, political, social and creative – are based on trust. Trust means that you can be trusted to take care of your own psycho-social-physical wellbeing and those of employees and clients in the carrying out of your professional responsibilities. Bullying, intimidation, threats, greed, arrogance, superiority and lack of transparency belie the practice of trust. In his inaugural speech, Ronald Reagan said that 'if you have not achieved governorship of your Self, how can you govern a country?' This is true for any individual who has a leadership or managerial role. It has not been incumbent on people who are given management roles to examine their own level of self-governorship, and this deficit in the selection and ongoing training of managers is a neglect of those managers, of their charges and, indeed, of the organisation itself. Males, in particular, shy away from examining their personal and interpersonal level of immaturity and this has not and does not bode well for the wellbeing of society, especially when eighty per cent of management power lies in males' hands – none more so than in the political, financial and health realms of our country.

It is the responsibility of each adult – no matter what their career status is – to look to take responsibility for self and for one's own actions. This examination is not a responsibility that can be benignly ignored; it is the essential means of becoming adult. Each one of us comes into our adult years carrying emotional baggage – inner uncertainties about ourselves – and the resolution of these insecurities is critical to the wellbeing of the said individual and the lives of all other individuals he or she encounters. The recovery of a strong sense of self, of one's unique individuality and of 'our power beyond measure' automatically leads to the recovery of seeing and valuing the individuality of others. This is true for parents, teachers, managers, politicians, health care professionals – indeed for all professionals.

Whether we like it or not, as adults our interiority totally determines what we feel, think, say and do; it particularly determines the nature of the relationship with others and the extent to which we take responsibility and are accountable for our own actions. When the government talked about replacing the heads of those banks that belied their clients' trust, I wondered what criteria they were using to determine the suitability of the replacements. A question that also needs to be asked is what level of maturity and self-governorship do those government ministers have who are overseeing the changes in the management of banks? The more individuals in leadership roles take on the responsibility of understanding themselves and create the opportunities and encouragement for others to do likewise, the greater the chance that a radical shift will occur in society that will benefit us all.

Take Note of Tone of Voice

Much of people's distress, particularly children's, arises in response to the tone of voice used by others. Many individuals are not conscious of the tone of voice they use but, nonetheless, conscious or not, they need to own what belongs to them. Contrary to what many people believe, tone of voice arises from an internal emotional place of either solidity or turmoil; when it is the former it communicates love, equality, openness, optimism, genuineness, sincerity, spontaneity, clarity, definitiveness and confidence; when it arises from inner turmoil it can communicate either in an acting-out way – aggression, irritability, tetchiness, dismissal, arrogance, control, dominance, hostility, threat, tension – or in an acting-in way – fearfulness, pessimism, passivity, sadness, uncertainty and indecisiveness. I used the phrase 'contrary to what many people believe' above as it is more commonly believed that it is somebody else that triggers the particular tone of voice used. However, the truth is that what comes from you is about you and it is a clever defensive manoeuvre to blame somebody else for your own responses. However, a defensive reaction never leads to a resolution of the underlying insecurity that gives rise to a defensive tone of voice. Whether we like it or not, our tone of voice at all times reveals – is a mirror of – our interiority.

It is an interesting exercise to brainstorm what are the possible tones of voice that we either use or encounter from others. Of course, having identified your own repertoire from the list below it behoves you to detect the inner source of the tones – particularly when they are of a defensive nature. The word 'tone' is an anagram of the word 'note' and for our own mature progress and the well-being of others, it is crucial for each of us to begin to consciously take note of our tone of voice.

In brainstorming, it is important to distinguish between the physical properties and the emotional intentions of tones of voice. For example, when I say 'your tone of voice is low', I am defining its physical sound but when I say 'your tone of voice is cross' I am alluding to its possible emotional intention to convey anger. I say 'possible' because it is crucial to check on your assumption and not presume you can read another person's behaviour. A mature enquiring would be to ask 'am I hearing anger in your voice?'

It is useful then to brainstorm two lists, one conveying what the tone sounds like and the other its possible emotional intention.

A tone of voice may sound light, heavy, squeaky, deep, high-pitched, low-pitched, deep-throated, light-airy, bellowing, whimpering, earthy, sharp, firm, flat, soft, well-modulated or full.

In terms of emotional intention, you may experience a tone of voice as cross, anxious, fearful, sad, depressed, joyful, chirpy, tentative, threatening, insistent, cutting, kind, gentle, tender, confident, indecisive, patronising, manipulative, domineering, rigid, seductive, flirtatious, erotic, mean, serious, ambivalent, vicious, sarcastic, cynical or dismissive.

As we can see, tone of voice is a powerful means of communication both for the person who is communicating and the person at the receiving end of the non-verbal message. In terms of the speaker, tone of voice offers a powerful window into his or her own interiority. In owning both aspects of voice tone, the speaker is given an opportunity to check the source of the tone, and when it is defensive in nature and expressing particular emergency feelings such as anger, sadness, fear, it provides the opportunity to strengthen one's inner stronghold of self. For example, if you notice your tone of voice is frequently cross, you may discover that the intention to convey anger was an attempt to get another person – adult or child – to take responsibility for some unmet need of yours, rather than you yourself take ownership of it. This happened to a teacher friend of mine who found that each day he went home from school feeling stressed and tired, he was cross with his five-year-old son, with whom his relationship had sadly deteriorated. He realised he was not looking after himself and that it was that neglect of himself he was projecting onto his unsuspecting, baffled and hurt son.

The person who is the target of another's tone of voice also has an opportunity to examine his or her present level of maturity. When a person personalises the other person's tone of voice – for example, 'that person's tone of voice' is not respectful of me – then there is an urgent enmeshment to be resolved. How is it that in the face say of a person's dismissive tone of voice you did not stay separate, hold onto your own worthy sense of self and enquire 'I feel that your tone of voice is being dismissive of yourself!' Recall that whether it is a non-verbal or verbal communication from another, the message is totally about the person sending the message and says absolutely nothing about you. When you receive it as being about you, it becomes necessary to work on your own relationship with yourself.

On Being Responsible

Many adults talk about the need for young people 'to be more responsible', possibly without reflecting on what is the true nature of responsibility.

There are two aspects to being responsible: one is the *owning* of your every feeling, thought, word and action; the other is having the *response-ableness* to follow through on your responsibilities. Response-ableness is not generally associated with being responsible, but how can any person who does not possess essential emotional, social and other life skills possibly be responsible in these areas of functioning? Whereas the nurturing of children is now more commonly accepted as critical to a child's security, the enablement of children can be missed as being equally important. Toddlers let us know the latter very definitely when they assert 'I want to do it myself'. It is now established that if parents want a responsible thirteen year old, then they need to start that process with the three-day-old. A response that toddlers need to hear ringing in their ears is not 'no', but 'just do it'. Clearly, parents will ensure there are no obvious dangers, but an anxious parent sees dangers where there are no dangers. The parent who overprotects children deprives them of the necessary opportunities to becoming confident and competent. Equally, the parent who dominates children with 'shoulds', 'have to's', 'ought to's', also undermines children's confidence and potential competence. Parents who are anxious or overprotect or live their lives through their children ('I do everything for the children') fail to show belief in their children's immense ability to gradually take charge of their own lives. In doing everything for children parents prevent them from learning to stand on their own two feet. Parents who dominate, control, have unrealistic expectations, push and are over-involved in their children's lives confuse their children with their achievements. Such confusion leads to a lack of confidence and an addiction to success. These children can become *over*-responsible in that they seek to please others, but patently neglect themselves. The essence of responsibility is to take care of self and own your responses, but children who are dominated see themselves as being owned by others. True responsibility is not within their remit.

A wise rule of thumb is 'do not do anything for a child that the child can do for self'. Another wise practice is the regular affirmation of each child's unique unlimited potential and the ingenious ways each child manifests his or her individuality. It still surprises me when parents answer the question 'what is it that draws you to love your baby?' with 'its helplessness'. Such a response is not a good start to developing a child's confidence, competence and responsibility. Babies many be dependent, but they are not one bit helpless; indeed, they are often far more powerful in voicing their needs than many adults. Children need to be loved for self and believed in and encouraged to explore the world they live in. It is crucial that those two responsibilities of parents and teachers be kept separate; any enmeshment creates emotional insecurity and blocks children's innate excitement for living, natural curiosity and eagerness to learn.

The aspect of responsibility with which most adults struggle is to own their own responses. We are extraordinary in the way we project responsibility for our feelings, words and action onto others:

- 'You made me angry'
- 'You deserved what I said'
- 'You drove me to hit you'.

Examples of passing the buck are multiple:

- 'You only think about yourself'
- 'You're a bully'
- 'You're a liar and a cheat'
- 'You think you're better than the rest of us'.

When you examine the above responses, what is clear is the absence of the 'I'. However, the central letter in the word respons-*i*-bility is 'I' and this demands that the person take ownership of his own responses and any action that such ownership demands. Take the example above of 'you made me angry'; responsibility here requires the 'I' message: 'I feel angry.' Anger is an energy provided for the person to mobilise him on some unmet need or unexpressed value or belief. Blaming another is looking to the other to take responsibility for your unmet need, but each of us is 100 per cent responsible for our own needs! If we had the good fortune to be reared in an environment where we were given daily opportunities to take responsibility for many of our own needs, as young and older adults, we would automatically own and take action on our own needs, beliefs and values. However, if we had been spoilt or over-protected or dominated, is it any wonder we act in ways that are in keeping with that rearing – 'passing the buck'? It is a much harder challenge to learn responsibility as an adult. Nevertheless, the responsibility lies with the adult – if they are in that place to do so – to ensure that children live in environments where being responsible is central to family, community and school wellbeing. Those adults who do not have the psycho-social readiness to create mature environments need to seek help to redress the situation – a critical act of responsibility!

The Path to Accountability

What has been most noticeable since the recession started three years ago is the major lack of accountability by individuals in the banks, government, property development, financial institutions and public bodies. Not one individual has stood up and admitted to the avarice, greed, corruption, unethical practices and depersonalising of staff members and customers that were part and parcel of their professional practice. Many of these individuals have attempted to hide behind the system – politicians are amazing at doing it – but it is not a system that neglects people, it is individuals. The whole sad lack of accountability is crying out for an explanation. Why would so many individuals who are well-educated, in status positions and possessing considerable political or financial power not own up to their very serious misdemeanours? It is not that those individuals – incidentally, mostly male – lack intelligence, but they certainly appear to lack maturity. If accountability was present we would have emerged from the economic recession much more quickly. The danger now is that if accountability does not emerge, any economic recovery will be built on the same defensive emotional/social foundations which led to the economic crash. I have found little evidence in the analysis of the causes of the recession that point to the very powerful emotional process that underpinned the economic collapse.

What is important to appreciate is that these powerful emotional processes are peculiar to individuals, and while at an external level we can point to the avarice, greed, self-centredness, depersonalisation, target-fixated mentality and betrayal of trust, there are deeper emotional realities to be detected. Unless these deeper, more hidden realities are identified by each of the individuals who were exploitative and reckless with the 'widow's mite', there will be no emergence of external accountability. When these individuals fail to examine their professional behaviour and do not come to realise that their 'unprofessional' conduct mirrors a deeper dark reality of personal insecurity, they will continue to blatantly rationalise their actions. When individuals do not have a consciousness of unresolved inner turmoil, they are unconsciously and automatically in defence and this defensiveness manifests itself in *denial*. Denial is a very powerful unconscious defence and arises from deep personal insecurity. Unless the confused identity that lies at the heart of the neglect of others is resolved, no external accountability is possible. The most common confusions that exist are the confusion of one's self and worth with such externals as power, wealth, status, success, prestige and work. Behind these projections lie fears of rejection and failure. Internal accountability is about becoming conscious of these inner unresolved conflicts and making new and mature responses to resolve them; when deep-seated and particularly when denial is present, professional psychotherapeutic help is required.

In terms of the prevention of the greed, avarice, bullying, depersonalisation, betrayal of trust and addictions to success, power, status and wealth that have haunted our society over the last two decades, it is vital that individuals who have positions of power – parental, political, educational, occupational, social, religious – be provided with the opportunities to closely examine their behaviour so that their inner turmoil is not projected onto others. In other words, personal development needs to be an integral part of professional development. The latter notion is critical to human wellbeing. Professional training courses need to incorporate examination of and deepening of personal maturity; too long it has been assumed that education and status equals personal maturity, but the reality is that age, status, education, gender or wealth are no indices of maturity. What *are* indices of maturity are a solid sense of self that is not tied to anything outside of self and a separateness and independence in one's relationship with others, work, creativity, wealth, productivity and success. It is a deep and complex process; the greatest impediments are a lack of regard for self, a lack of confidence in one's intelligence beyond measure and the illusion that something outside self will resolve one's inner turmoil. Internal accountability for our own insecurities is fundamental to accountability for the external actions that have so belied the trust that is inherent in professionalism.

The Uncomfortable Challenge of Accountability

It is now generally accepted that those in positions of power during the 'boom' times – in governments, banks, other financial institutions, property development – did not exhibit mature management or leadership. The position is quite clear; either they knew what was going on and didn't do anything about it or they didn't know what was going on and, thereby, were not up to the jobs they were in. Either way, in any crisis – and this has been major and has drastically affected people's lives and may be a factor in the observed twenty-five per cent dramatic increase in suicide – there is an opportunity to learn from what has happened and set the solid foundations for future emotional, social and economic wellbeing for *all* citizens here and, indeed, elsewhere. I emphasise 'all' because what has emerged is that a dark narcissism had deeply infected the actions of the major players in the economic upturn and downturn.

There is a large stumbling block to learning from the mistakes made and that is a great reluctance on the part of the main players to reflect on their actions or lack of actions and to be accountable for same. There appears to be an entrenched position in there being no accountability. Admittedly, there is a drive towards introducing more regulation but regulation does not create the individual maturity, authenticity and independence that is critical to accountability. Neither does regulation guarantee accountability.

Furthermore, it was individuals who acted wrongly – not systems – and unless these individuals take up the urgent call in the crisis for mature reflection, the problem is far more serious than presently being portrayed. There is the equally serious consideration that if reflection and accountability are not forthcoming, it has to be questioned whether or not those who have retained their managerial and leadership positions are truly up to the responsibilities of their jobs. I truly wonder that if these individuals were asked to define maturity would they include authenticity, independence and accountability in their definition.

There is another question abegging – how is it that those individuals who held so much power do not possess the maturity to honestly address their role in what has transpired? These persons – mostly male – are highly educated, knowledgeable, wealthy, of an age where you would expect a wisdom of years, have (or had) huge status and wielded considerable power. However, none of these achievements or qualities is an index of maturity. Maturity automatically involves being authentic, independent and accountable, and I believe it is here where the crux lies. How many of the individuals concerned can claim to possess any of these essential human qualities?

Leaders and managers – like the rest of us – have their stories, and when you have not examined your own story and retained the openness and replaced the defences of earlier years with mature openness, beliefs, attitudes, values and actions, you are likely to continue to operate out from defensive places. In the training of managers and leaders it has not been seen as essential that they know and understand themselves first before they take on their highly responsible roles. There are four critical inner examinations required:

- Am I independent of what I do, of what I achieve and of how others perceive and respond to me?
- Do I own all my words and actions as mine and take due accountability when things go 'right' *and* when things go 'wrong'?

- Do I operate from a place of authenticity, most especially when either I let myself or others down?
- Do I seek the professional help needed to resolve my defensive ways that are blocks to my personal, interpersonal and professional progress?

You may have noticed that I put the words 'right' and 'wrong' in quotes, the reason being that I believe people are not consciously superior, greedy, narcissistic, aggressive or success addicted but operate out unconsciously from these defensive places. However, whether or not your actions are consciously or unconsciously taken, you are accountable and that brings us back to precisely where we started.

When it comes to independence, how many of those who hold the reins of financial and political power can claim to be independent and not define themselves and their worth by any of the following – status, achievements, work, success, power and wealth? When you are dependent and have a deep fear of falling off your pedestal you will have a vested interest in not being accountable. Resolution is only possible when fear gives way to fearlessness and dependence to independence. And when it comes to authenticity – how many can put their hands on their hearts and declare that 'I am always real in what I say and do' in the face of possible responses from others of judgement, criticism, witch-hunts, ridicule, violence and condemnation? The reality is that no real progress is possible without authenticity.

East Meets West on Stress Reduction

The relief of stress is a multi-billion euro industry. A cough, a cold, a headache and a stomach ache sends the sufferer scurrying to the medicine cabinet or pharmacy in search of 'a cure'. There are over-counter medications that either lead to the digestive tract slowing down or speeding up, others to relieve heartburn or neutralise excess stomach acid. There are prescription drugs available to reduce anxiety – Valium, Xanax. There are multiple pain killers available and Tagamet and Zantac that decrease the secretion of stomach acid are frequently prescribed. There are anti-depressants available for alterations in mood. The problem with the widespread use of many such medications is that, even though the symptoms are temporarily alleviated, the underlying issues – physical, psychological, social or spiritual – that are producing the symptoms may not be getting addressed. Symptoms arise to tell us that something is out of balance. If we ignore these messages or, more alarmingly, suppress them, it may only lead to more severe symptoms and a deepening of the unresolved underlying issues. What is more disturbing about people's reliance on medication is that they become dependent on them and do not learn how to listen and trust their bodies. An alternative approach to drug cures is direly needed – and such an approach is available. Fifteen years ago a stress-reduction clinic was set up at the University of Massachusetts Medical Center by Dr Jon Kabat-Zinn. It is an eight-week programme and consists of eight two-hour classes plus a one-day workshop. The course is called Mindfulness-Based Stress Reduction (MBSR) and is based on the essential teaching of well-know Buddhist figures such as Thich Nhat Hahn and Eckhart Tolle. Mindfulness is more than a meditation practice that can have profound medical and psychological benefits; it is also a way of life that reveals the tender and loving wholeness that lies at the heart of our being, even in times of great pain and suffering. The MBSR course is a unique synthesis of East and West – of meditation and yoga with science and mainstream medicine.

The individuals who attended the courses over the last fifteen years were referred by their doctors for a wide range of medical conditions – headaches, high blood pressure, back pain, heart disease, cancer and AIDS. What these people learned during the course was the *how* of taking care of themselves – not a replacement for their medical treatment, but a vitally important complement to it. A particularly helpful part of the Mindfulness-Based Stress Reduction Programme is that attendees are taught body consciousness and a body scan method that enables them to get to know their own bodies. The course emphasises that in training people to listen to their bodies, they make intelligent decisions about obtaining medical attention for any identified pain or discomfort. The work of mindfulness is always carried out in conjunction with all the medical treatments that may be required to relieve pain. It is not meant to be a substitute for it but can be a vital complement to medical treatment.

The question that needs to be asked regarding the MBSR course is: does it work? The evidence to date suggests quite a dramatic therapeutic effect. Before individuals begin the programme they fill out a questionnaire in which they identify from a list of over one hundred common physical and emotional symptoms those they have experienced in the preceding month. They repeat this exercise at the end of the course. The average number of symptoms out of the hundred is twenty-two. When people finish the course the average drops to fourteen – showing an average reduction of thirty-six per cent. This is a dramatic change over a short duration, especially for people who have had these symptoms over a long period of time. What is even more reassuring is that several follow-up studies indicate that the improvements gained were maintained. Indeed, most participants rate their training as very important to their improved wellbeing. All in all, the course has considerable therapeutic effects on such conditions as stress, chronic pain, anxiety and panic, headaches, back pain, high blood pressure, psoriasis, acne, insomnia, fatigue.

The good news is that the MBSR course is now available in Ireland and is being offered by several highly trained practitioners throughout the country.

The Place of Dignity and Compassion in the Medical Care of People

The British government has launched a 'dignity and care' campaign with 4,500 National Health Service (NHS) health care staff; the plans are to provide training courses on compassion for these employees. It would not surprise me if the Health Service Executive (HSE) takes up on the NHS's initiative. Surveys within the NHS have shown that many health care personnel view their medical duties as a series of mechanical tasks rather than a series of human interactions. This lack of compassion and denying of dignity for individuals who are ill and distressed are viewed as having a counter-therapeutic effect. Indeed, the research findings suggest that dignity and compassion may have an even greater therapeutic effect than the actual medical therapies or surgeries being carried out. This claim is not new – bedside manner has always been seen as critical to the medical care of a person.

While treating symptoms is necessary, thoughtfulness and care are also needed to help someone truly feel better. Indeed, Professor Hugh McKenna of Ulster University has asserted that within the complex maze of health services what is needed are staff members who are prepared to enter into relationship with their clients and to foster hope rather than hopelessness. The British NHS in its constitution has listed compassion as one of its core values and it pledges that staff 'find the time to listen and talk when it is needed, make the effort to understand, and get on and do the small things that mean so much – not because we are asked to but because we care'. The NHS is determined to find ways of measuring compassionate caring. In my view, the qualities of compassionate care are:

- relating to the person as a unique individual worthy of care and attention
- understanding that illness has a unique meaning for each person
- listening attentively to how they describe their illness and their needs around it
- showing patience and kindness at all times and apologising when one is impatient
- responding empathically to the person's emotional responses to their illness – fear, sadness, depression, uncertainty, insecurity, terror, guilt.

The French philosopher Jean-Jacques Rousseau sums up compassion very well when he says that 'there is no greater wisdom than human kindness'.

However, the emphasis on there being 'a pill for every ill', on routines and systems and the pressures on the health services have eroded the place of heart in the medical care of individuals. However, what the NHS in Britain do not seem to be addressing is, one, that health care personnel are very much at risk themselves when they are not compassionate in the carrying out of their duties and, two, that many health care employees do not experience compassion from their managers in their interactions with them. For example, stress-related illness and absenteeism are high among the major body of health care personnel – nurses – and yet there does not appear to be the presence of any effort on the part of managers to compassionately respond to this worrying phenomenon. For example, a nurse related to me her experience of having missed work due to a stress-related illness. On her return to work she was called to the nurse manager's office and told that her absenteeism was not acceptable. When she protested about the levels of stress she and other nurses were under, she was told she needed to go to the Employment Assistance Officer to learn 'better coping skills'. It appears to me that it is the manager who needs to learn more effective and compassionate managerial skills! These managers might defend themselves by saying that they, too, are under pressure from their own managers to have staff on wards and in specialist units. However, nurses could engage the same defence by asserting that they are under pressure within what appears to be a highly mismanaged national health service.

When staff or managers are under pressure, resolution of these pressures is required. It is a bit much to now ask health care staff to go on courses on how to be compassionate in their profession. Don't take me up wrongly here. I believe the proposed training is vital for an effective health service but if 'charity starts at home', so does compassion. When health care personnel are not compassionate in the carrying out of their duties, it is important to see that this deficit puts not only their clients at risk, but also themselves. I believe it is in our nature to love and when that is repressed or suppressed in daily work practices then the health care person is now 'psychologically' distressed and may well have accompanying embodiments of that inner turmoil.

I do hope – because it was not directly expressed – that the training in compassionate caring will be offered to all health care professionals, in particular managers and medical consultants who, sadly, are notoriously known for their lack of compassionate responding. Incidentally, compassionate responding is not just a responsibility for those of us who work in the area of health care; it is also a responsibility for individuals working in all professions – education, finance, industry, politics, etc.

Meditation or Medication: That is the Question

I spent a fascinating weekend in Killarney at a very special and innovative Conference on Mindfulness and Palliative Care. The idea of such a conference being held in Ireland, even within the last five years, would not have been envisaged. There were interesting speakers at the conference, most notably Sogyal Rinpoche, author of *The Tibetan Book of Living and Dying*, and Jon Kabat-Zinn, author of several books, most notably *Full Catastrophe Living*. Our own Tony Bates also brought a special presence and maturity to the conference as did several other Irish speakers.

Over 450 health care professionals attended the conference and I felt, alongside myself, that they were inspired not only by what was being said but by the energy of presence and of love that radiated from both the presenters and the participants.

Jon Kabat-Zinn made a crucial reference to the latter experience when he said, 'You risk losing professional credibility with your colleagues when you mention love.' Taking this statement a step further, those who recoil at the mention of 'love' are more in need of help than the individuals they are helping. The deepest need of each and every human being is to be unconditionally loved and the ignoring and dismissal of that fundamental need lies at the root of much that is dis-eased within our health service system and within other social, work and educational systems. When a medical professional does not therapeutically respond to the whole person, he is operating from a disconnection from his own amazing and unique nature. Without the above considerations, Jon Kabat-Zinn did say that it is often the case that 'the health care professionals need more help than their patients!'

One of the central themes of the conference was the practice of meditation, and the research findings demonstrate that for many 'medical' conditions meditation is four times more effective than medication! There was also the enlightening point made by Sogyal Rinpoche that 'when medicine is ineffective, compassion is always effective'.

It appears to me that there are two kinds of meditation – one is the kind you practise alone, in private and the other is the one we bring to our therapeutic and medical practice. My most profound experiences have arisen from being totally present to the person seeking my help. Being totally present to the person's presence is truly meditation as a living and loving practice. Such a powerful meeting with the other person's presence embraces not only total focus and love, but also compassion for the pain, illness or misery that the person is enduring. It would seem that many health care professionals would benefit enormously from meditation and compassionate practice. This echoes the words of the French philosopher Pascale, that 'all man's problems arise from the inability to sit in a room by himself'. The words of Francis W. Peabody, Harvard Medical School, add further weight to the foregoing: 'The secret of the care of the patient is in caring for the patient.' Actually, Peabody could have added that 'the secret of the care of the patient is in the health practitioner caring for self so that he can more effectively care for the patient'. Even the term 'patient' needs to be dropped and replaced by the word 'person'. The word 'patient' depersonalises and disempowers individuals and I believe, only exacerbates the very difficulties for which they are seeking help. Given, too, that everything we say is about ourselves, at an unconscious level, the label 'patient' used by health practitioners may indeed symbolically represent the need to be 'patient' with self and with those individuals who seek our help! Curiously, 'patience', a virtue that is critical to parenting, teaching, child-minding, psychological counselling, psychotherapy, psychoanalysis, managing, medical and social work practices, is a word or practice rarely mentioned in relevant professional literature.

Of course, charity and compassion begin at home and the nature and caring of another is totally determined by a professional's inner relationship with self. There is also the dire necessity that the culture of the health service is of a nature that actively promotes the compassionate care of each individual staff member and that fiscal and system pressures do not jeopardise that essential relating. The present recession has highlighted how the powerful emotional forces of depersonalisation and de-individualisation, coupled with a profit-target-fixated mentality and loss of trust led to blind greed, avarice and an absence of dignifying relationships with staff, clients, shareholders and communities.

Politicians have a critical role to play in this development of compassionate care. It is going to be a very hard lesson for individuals who head health, fiscal, industrial and service organisations to value themselves and others before profits, but I do believe it is the only way forward.

7 Training for Consciousness

When individual leaders and managers operate from unconscious defensive places then what they defensively feel, think, say and do poses a threat to the wellbeing of their peers, subordinates and family members and, indeed, to the organisation in which they have a leadership role. The belief in the literature and in corporate practice that the 'highly engaged' leaders and managers need to be retained with outlandish cash bonuses has seriously been brought into question. In any case, the bonuses did not work; if they had we would not have suffered such a devastating recession. The assumption was that the highly engaged leaders and managers were mature, but all the signs are that they were very frightened individuals as evidenced in their addiction to success, fear of failure, depersonalisation of themselves and employees, reckless competitiveness, secretiveness and the formation of cosy cartels, not to mention bullying, arrogance, superiority, greed, avarice and narcissism.

All of these signs of immaturity are unconscious defences driven by powerful emotional processes. What we require are leaders and managers who are engaged and committed to their work. Such balanced leadership springs from a deep personal engagement with self, a consciousness of a solid interiority, from an independence and separateness from achievements and success and a deep realisation that the progress of an organisation depends on a commitment to upholding the dignity of employees and customers.

Opportunities to realise one's maturity need to be made available on an ongoing basis, not only for leaders and managers, but for all staff members. Maturation is not optional, it is a profound responsibility, but is only likely to emerge under certain personal, interpersonal and organisational circumstances. No leader or manager or employee wants to remain hidden behind defensive walls but, depending on the frequency, intensity and duration of the threats to authentic expression, it can take considerable efforts to bring about a shift from unconsciousness to consciousness and from defensive to authentic action. However, rest assured that such a shift benefits everybody and the work organisation. An employee who feels individualised, believed in, empowered and respected will be loyal to the work organisation and committed to his work responsibilities. However, it appears to demand considerable effort to convince those who hold positions of status and power that a happy, contented employee is an organisation's best asset, as, indeed, is a happy, contented customer. Inevitably, what is blocking those in leadership roles from understanding these fundamental facts is their own unconscious fears and insecurities which are masked by innumerable powerful defences. The requirements are, one, to create training opportunities for those in leadership and managerial roles that will create a shift in consciousness and, two, to get those individuals – particularly males – to embrace the opportunity.

What is absent in most work and political organisations is a mechanism that challenges individuals who occupy top leadership and managerial positions. It is often very threatening for those in middle-management to be authentic and real with their managers and the lack of invitation to provide feedback means that immature actions, values and practices go unchallenged. Somehow, it needs to be integral to the professional development of those in power positions to be exposed to an examination of their current governing practices for the sake of their own wellbeing as well as that of other employees. When governors are open to reflection on an ongoing training basis, they act as models for other employees, very much in the same way as a parent can do for children and a teacher for students. It would also be beneficial to provide training to deepen personal maturity for all staff members so that everybody is singing from the same hymn sheet.

Training for Raising Consciousness

There is a very powerful and sensitive process involved in creating a shift from the genius of unconsciousness to the genius of consciousness, from operating from a defensive world to an open, transparent, real and authentic world. Some individuals can achieve some shifts following an illness or a tragedy, from attending a seminar, reading books on the subject or from an enlightened friend or colleague. However, in most cases what is required is an intensive face-to-face training that becomes integral to professional development. The face-to-face training needs to be done by professionals who have a deep understanding of human behaviour and human relationships, of unconsciousness and consciousness and who live and breathe what they teach. The process involves:

- identifying unconscious processes
- helping each individual governor to become *conscious* of those processes as they emerge in an interactive setting
- the development of a compassionate understanding of how the defensive behaviours uncovered have been created in response to threats experienced from early childhood and onwards
- the emergence, as realization heightens, of new choices, new ways of being affective and effective in relationship with self, peers, other employees, family members and the work organisation
- engagement in the authentic actions that follow on from the new choices.

Given the differences in each person's story, the time frame for the above process is different for each individual. What is crucial is the level of emotional, intellectual, behavioural, social and creative safety created by the trainer.

- *Emotional* safety is the modelling of and the giving of permission for emotional expression and emotional receptivity to each person in the training group.

- *Intellectual* safety involves the affirmation of the genius of each person and the resolution of the common confusion of knowledge with intelligence. What is also important is the restoration of failure and success to being intrinsic to work and learning and the focusing on progress as a personal and organisational goal.
- *Behavioural* safety is brought about through illustrating how each and every human behaviour is creative and its intention is always for the wellbeing of the person.
- *Social* safety is the affirming of the unique presence and, indeed, absence of each person in the group. Individuality is especially emphasized.
- *Creative* safety is the non-judgemental acknowledgement of each person's creative responses to challenges and the embracing of difference as opportunity rather than conflict.

Step One: Identifying Unconscious Processes

In a ground-breaking book, *The Talent Masters*, the authors Bill Conaty and Ram Charan capture the essence of the power of the unconscious to influence the actions of leaders and managers:

> Your drive, your psychological likes and dislikes, your motives to achieve goals, and the values by which you achieve those goals are all part of the emotional etchings buried in your inner core. They shape the way you make decisions, exercise judgement, and take action. They affect the people who come into contact with you: subordinates, peers, family. They affect how you see these people. Your inner core determines how clearly you see and perceive, what you select as important, how you think and act, and the quality of your judgements, decision, and relationships. It affects the way you frame an issue, how you search for information, and from whom. And it very often does these things without Tweeting them to your conscious mind.
>
> Becoming aware of and dealing with your inner core is at the centre of leadership effectiveness and development. The more acutely you're aware of it, the better you will be as a leader.

What is fascinating is that individuals reveal their unconscious etchings all the time, not just through Freudian slips of the tongue but by the presence of, or, more often than not, the absence of either welfare or emergency feelings, by body posture, by tone of voice, by facial expression, by the words they employ and by their interactions with others. For example, a threatening tone of voice accounts for much of human misery and reveals underlying feelings, attitudes and beliefs that need to come to the surface. Only the person himself can reveal what it is that is causing him to, say, be aggressive in his tone of voice. Raising consciousness of what is unconscious demands for the trainer to create the emotional, intellectual and social safety for the leader or manager to uncover what is hidden from his conscious mind. If the individual leader or manager senses any threat to being authentic – for example, criticism, judgement – they will cleverly resort to another defensive response and the opportunity for consciousness is lost. What needs to be understood is that no leader or manager wants to operate from defensive places but it takes a considerably raised consciousness on the part of the mentor, whether working one-to-one or with a group, to create a climate that is unconditional, compassionate, non-judgemental and supportive.

Most recruitment companies tend to use tests to identify what they call likes and dislikes, strengths and weaknesses and positives and negatives. It is my understanding that, as human beings, we are not weak or 'negative' but we are defensive for very good reasons. Stopping at the surface of so-called strengths and weaknesses misses out on the very powerful unconscious possibilities that, when brought to consciousness, can result in seismic changes.

Aggression and bullying are common manifestations of unconscious processes and are a serious liability in terms of employees' wellbeing and motivation but also in the making of key governing decisions. Aggression and bullying often mask, for example, fears of failure, addiction to success, status anxiety, an over-powering drive to dominate and control and a fear of not being good enough. Whatever the source, unless it becomes conscious and resolved, then personal, professional and organisational progress can be seriously interrupted.

The reality is, that like most of us, leaders and managers have blind spots that shadow their wholeness, create an inner imbalance and a jaundiced view of other people's behaviour. Raising consciousness is aimed at bringing to light these blind spots so that the leader better knows self, can be affirming, effectively evaluate situations, motivate and inspire employees and have an understanding of what motivates himself, his peers, other employees and customers.

In the process of raising consciousness there is no more reliable access to what lies hidden than the feelings that leaders and managers experience. Because of the way males are reared, most leaders and managers repress or suppress their emotions and attempt to block, stifle and dismiss emotional expression in others. Identifying feelings is the first step, followed by 'how is it that I am feeling this way?' For example, if a leader is feeling angry, then an enquiry into the source of that feeling is crucial: 'how is it that I'm feeling angry?' and 'what is the intention of this feeling?' Feelings arise as resources about and for the person experiencing them; when they are projected onto others – 'you make me angry' – then a defensive dance is likely to follow. Anger is an energy that alerts to some action you need to take for self, not against another. For instance, the manager who frequently bullies may be masking a need to be master of his own ship but doubts his ability to do this. What has defensively worked for him – to the detriment of others – is to overpower others.

With regard to female managers, generally speaking, women are regarded as being more emotionally literate than men. However, their emotional literacy tends to be focused on rescuing those who are emotionally distressed rather than empowering them in an empathic way to take responsibility for the messages that their feelings bring for conscious consideration. Furthermore, while women are more comfortable sitting with the welfare and emergency emotions of another, they frequently are poor at identifying their own feelings and taking conscious responsibility for them. The training of female managers needs to be alert to these emotional repressions

and provide the relationship safety for what is emotionally unconscious to become conscious.

In mentoring, emotional responses offer the most potent opportunities to access the unconscious.

Step Two: Raising Consciousness of What Has Been Identified

Once defensive responses have been identified it is then necessary
to further raise the consciousness of what has led to the adoption of
these masked responses. Certainly, the frequency, intensity and
endurance in the present and over time of the threats experienced
are important indicators of how embedded are these unconscious
creations. For example, if passivity is identified, then it is likely that
the person's censoring of his tongue goes right back to childhood to
either an overbearing, hypercritical parent or teacher or both. Inci-
sive and sensitive enquiry is required to unearth the rejection, pain
and hurt that led to the development of passivity. It is not an
uncommon belief in work organisations that 'if you are going to say
anything, say nothing'. When individual governors get to the roots of
their defensive feelings, thoughts, words and actions, consciously
appreciate the creativity and intelligence of these responses and avail
of the opportunity here and now to free themselves of their con-
straints, there is generated a psycho-social energy that transforms
their personal and interpersonal abilities.

A powerful aid to raising consciousness is relevant self-disclosure
on the part of the mentor, which can often create a level playing
field in terms of authentic expression and accountability. Equally,
when a peer is open about his defences, others find the emotional
safety to allow a deepening of consciousness to emerge; this is one
of the powers of a group dynamic. Nevertheless, there is no hard
and fast rule when it comes to human beings shifting from unconsciousness to consciousness and it needs to be the choice of the
individual leader as to what best works for him – a one-to-one
meeting or group dynamic or a combination of both.

Step Three: The Development of Compassionate Understanding

It is my belief that human beings do not deliberately and consciously harm others; on the contrary, what are perceived by others as their 'bad', 'evil', 'selfish', 'narcissistic' actions are all unconscious attempts to prevent harm to themselves. As long as we continue to defensively judge others, then no progress in human relations can be made. Indeed, those who judge and witch-hunt others are also operating from unconscious defensive places and are in need of as much help as those whom they malign. Our nature is good and when it is held unconditionally and non-judgementally, our individual wholeness expresses itself in the very ways it has been held. This understanding of human behaviour is not an attempt to excuse it; on the contrary, the process of raising consciousness is to bring about a conscious responsibility towards care and empowerment of self and others. It is the experience of defensive relating on the part of significant others that led us when children to form defensive responses; then, when adults, it is open, authentic, unconditional and non-judgemental relating on the part of significant others that will bring about and reinforce consciousness of individual wholeness.

Compassion arises when a conscious awareness is reached of not only what we had to do as children in order to survive the defences of others, but also of the loss of love, understanding and empowerment that we deserved but, unfortunately, did not receive. There is also compassion needed for the feelings of fear, terror, upset, depression and guilt that dare not be expressed and the hiding of the different physical, sexual, emotional, intellectual, behavioural, social, creative and spiritual violations experienced. It is one of the most poignant moments of raising consciousness when an individual makes connections with what he has buried and masked, and the flow of emotion from him and others in the group is both uplifting and transformational. When the private world of individual managers emerges, a powerful bonding occurs between the members of the group. Fortunately, we now live in a

culture where people are more willing to talk about their inne
feelings, thoughts, dreams and personal aspects of their lives. Thi
is in contrast to a situation where business people were hugely
reluctant to talk about their inner worlds. Certainly, the more
understanding and compassion is present, the safer it is for indi
viduals to allow us enter into their interior worlds.

Step Four: Making New Conscious Choices

As individual leaders and managers come into a deeper and com
passionate consciousness of their defensive actions to date, new
choices emerge, not only in their professional lives but in their per
sonal and interpersonal relationships as well. A common revelation
for many leaders and managers is an addiction to work and to
success leading to the neglect of their own and employees' welfare
and, if married, of their spouses and, where there are offspring, o
their children. This is both a powerful awakening and a painful real
isation, but it leads to mature decisions regarding themselves
employees, the work organisation, their spouses and their children
Be assured that these new decisions benefit everybody, including the
organisation. Organisations that do not provide opportunities for
their leaders and managers to develop conscious insight into their
own and other employees' defensive responses that manifest in
defensive attitudes, values, beliefs and behaviours waste precious
potential. In a one-to-one mentoring situation the individual leader
would be encouraged and supported to begin to list new choices
and in a group situation, each participant to begin to list identified
defences, what lies hidden behind them and what new choices can
be made. Because we wear a thousand masks, the unmasking often
starts with the least and moves gradually to the greater hurts experienced. Because trust was lost in homes and classrooms and
considerable threats exist within the work organisation, individual
leaders and managers wisely dip their toe in the sea of trust before
they eventually plunge into the depths of trusting themselves and no
longer entrusting the care of self to others.

The kinds of processes involved in making authentic choices are:

- being present to one's interiority
- maintaining separateness from what others feel, think, say and do
- reclaiming one's life as being there for oneself
- taking conscious charge
- synthesis of head and heart, of feelings and thoughts
- experimenting
- taking conscious responsibility for self.

Step Five: Conscious New Actions

It is one thing for a leader or manager to identify new choices he needs to make; it is an entirely different matter to enact these choices. Indeed, the time gap between step four and five can be quite long, because the threats that led to masking what is authentic are often still present in some form or other, and the risk of rejection, humiliation, demeaning and lessening of one's presence is high. Wisely, the person holds back until he has established a more solid interiority, independence and, especially, separateness from the words and actions of others. Belonging first to one's own interiority is an essential foundation to maturity, and from that inner stronghold to not internalise the defences of others and to proceed to authentic actions. It is for the individual or group facilitator to support each leader or manager to examine their relationship with self, to identify where this is defensive and to encourage the expression of whatever aspect of self that lies hidden behind the defence. It is in this way that personal effectiveness is the basis for professional effectiveness and the evaluation of the personal maturity of managers in a face-to-face training situation becomes critical for organisational effectiveness.

Training for consciousness needs to be a re-occurring aspect of professional development. When managers are deeply defended the conscious uncovering of these defences is a sensitive, gradual and time-demanding exercise. The frequency of the face-to-face training sessions will be determined by the levels of defensiveness of the individual managers. Rest assured that ongoing work will be required.

Finally, in terms of the training of managers and leaders, there follows an outline of what would constitute the learning objectives of such training:

1. To have a conscious insight into the nature of the unconscious and its effects on managerial leadership and the organisation

2. To explore his understanding of the *nature of person and behaviour* so that his attitudes towards self, staff members and customers are person-centred rather than target or performance fixated

3. To bring to conscious awareness his own substitute/defensive responses and to know what new choices and actions need to be taken in the face of these blocks to personal, professional and organisational progress

4. To engender the ability to develop relationships with staff that are of an *affirming* and *empowering* nature

5. To develop the skills to effectively create the physical, sexual, emotional, intellectual, behavioural, social and creative safeties for employees to maximise their potential

6. To possess the skills to *proact* (rather than react) when confronted with employee/customer substitute/defensive responses

7. To possess the clear knowledge that affectiveness is the basis for effectiveness, as personal effectiveness is the basis for professional effectiveness

8. To develop the skills to listen and communicate in ways that enhance relationship and employee motivation and creativity

9. To discover how the quiet suffocation of individuality in employees and customers that emerged over the past decade can be undone

10. To work with conflict as opportunity to deepen relationships and enhance employee motivation and effectiveness

Management with Consciousness: An Overview

The recession has brought to light the darkness of the narcissism, individualism, greed, avarice, depersonalisation and denial that has crippled many national economies. There developed a quiet suffocation of individuality, authenticity and accountability in many workplaces – most notably financial institutions and health services. Furthermore, the target-fixated mentality in many multinationals led to serious depersonalisation of employees and the emergence of an unprecedented level of bullying and passivity.

One of the great crimes in the area of management was the development of human resources departments. The word resource took the 'person and heart' out of managing employees and reflected the prevailing attitude in many companies of 'profit before people'. It comes as no surprise that complaints of bullying are commonplace in the workplace and that many managers believe that the way to motivate employees is to bully them. The devastating effects of bullying on children, not only by their peers but by significant adults in their lives, are well documented. The effects on employees is also becoming more and more documented and many work organisations are facing legal challenges to allowing a bullying type of management operate within the workplace.

It is critical that leaders of work organisations learn to appreciate that it is not human resources but individual persons they employ, not only for the welfare of their employees or the creation of a wellness ethos, but also to improve effectiveness, affectiveness, efficiency and productivity. An employee who is respected, individualised and enabled is far more motivated and committed than the employee who complains of anonymity or being bullied. It may appear simple to say, but a happy and contented employee is a much greater asset to any organisation than an employee who harbours aggressive or passive-aggressive resentment.

It is a responsibility of organisations and individual managers to ensure that the quality of management is of a nature that enhances relationship and enables employees. However, such maturity is only possible when individual managers and supervisors possess a high level of personal maturity. Professional effectiveness is largely determined by personal effectiveness. However, it has not been the policy of work organisations and employers to evaluate the interiority of their managers. This is a serious oversight because the manager who carries considerable emotional baggage into the workplace can wreak havoc with relationships and create a dark work ethos. Just as parents and teachers, who are people-managers of homes and classrooms respectively, are the architects of their domains, so too are managers the architects of staff morale. Professional qualifications, gender, age, status and wealth are no indices of emotional and social maturity and it is incumbent on employers and managers themselves that they reflect on their own level of personal maturity in order to be more effective in people-managing. It is equally important that there are structures in place that provide the opportunities for their managers to examine how they are within themselves and with others.

People-managing is not then just about management strategies and techniques; such approaches are not fully effective unless they spring from the manager's solid and wise interiority. As suggested above, a very definite responsibility of managers is to develop an understanding of what happens within themselves and between themselves and employees. Managers effectively need training to come into consciousness in order to understand their own inner feelings as well as their inner and outer defensive responses and from that mature place they can better understand and respond maturely to the challenging behaviours of employees. It is with the defensive responses of self and employees that managers are especially challenged. The understanding of these defensive behaviours (for example, verbal aggression, non-cooperation, irresponsibility, passivity, poor motivation, stress reactions) is critical to effective management. The task of the manager is to get behind his own and employees' defensive reactions and focus on what lies hidden. More often than not, what is being masked are issues of low self-esteem, suppression of emotions, difficult staff relationships and

depersonalisation of employees. In the understanding
lenging behaviours there is no suggestion here to dilute the
and the influence on self and others of difficult human responses.
On the contrary, it is only by speaking the truth that real progress
can be made in determining the whys and wherefores of human
reactions. Nevertheless, the interpretations shown need to be non-
judgemental and empathic; otherwise understanding would be
threatening rather than enlightening in nature.

It is the responsibility of each of us to reflect on how we are
within ourselves and how we relate to others. For those in positions
of leadership and management, the need to reflect daily is even more
urgent since the influence wielded can have lasting effects on the
wellbeing and potential of others and on organisational effectiveness.
It is vital that leaders of work organisations, regardless of size,
provide the structures and positive climate for this review process.

A list of what I would consider to be the qualities of leadership
with consciousness follows and both a personal and interpersonal
checking of the presence or absence of these qualities is recommended.

Qualities of Leadership with Consciousness

Please tick each statement that is true for you.

1   Energetic __
2   Decisive __
3   Take responsibility for own actions and decisions __
4   Confident __
5   Have a clear vision of how the workplace needs to be __
6   Assertive __
7   Enable workers to reach their full potential __
8   Learn from past mistakes __
9   Firm on accountability __
10 Empower __

11   Consult with others __
12   Flexible __
13   Foster group decision making __
14   Persistent __
15   Consistent __
16   Challenge __
17   Confront when necessary __
18   Believe in the potential of employees __
19   Practise direct and clear communications __
20   Keen observer of behaviour __
21   Just and fair __
22   Take risks __
23   Committed __
24   Set clear boundaries __
25   Competent __
26   Efficient __
27   Appreciate difference __
28   Insightful __
29   Emotionally expressive __
30   Emotionally receptive __
31   Actively listen __
32   Trustworthy __
33   Nurture __
34   Considerate of the person, marriage and family __
35   Kind __
36   Love work __
37   Caring __
38   Respectful __
39   Affirming __
40   Fearless __
41   Loyal __
42   Empathic __
43   Compassionate __

44 Encouraging __

45 Supportive __

46 Seek support __

47 Spontaneous __

48 In touch with own inner issues __

49 Ability to comfort those in distress __

50 Know Self __

51 Inspirational __

52 Balanced lifestyle __

53 Dynamic __

54 Effectively resolve conflict/problems __

55 Independent and cooperative __

56 Open to feedback __

57 Creative __

58 Innovative __

59 Effective __

60 Realistic __

61 Appreciative __

62 Acknowledge all contributions __

63 Apologise when wrong __

64 Approachable __

64 Available __

66 Reflective __

67 Humorous __

68 Optimistic __

69 Know about employees' lives __

70 Congruent __

71 Recognise the individuality of each employee __

72 Show understanding __

73 Make requests – not order __

74 Authentic __

For A Leader

May you have the grace and wisdom
to act kindly, learning
To distinguish between what is
Personal and what is not.

May you be hospitable to criticism.

May you never put yourself at the centre of things.

May you act not from arrogance but out of service.

May you work on yourself,
Building up and refining the ways of your mind.

May those who work for you know
You see and respect them.

May you learn to cultivate the art of presence
In order to engage with those who meet you.

When someone fails or disappoints you,
May the graciousness with which you engage
Be their stairway to renewal and refinement.

. . . May you know the wisdom of deep listening.
The healing of wholesome words,
The encouragement of the appreciative gaze,
The decorum of held dignity.
The springtime edge of the bleak question.

May you have a mind that loves frontiers
So that you can evoke the bright fields
That lie beyond the view of the regular eye.

May you have good friends
To mirror your blind spots.

May leadership be for you
A true adventure of growth.

John O'Donohue (*Benedictus*)

Leabharlanna Fhine Gall

References

Central Statistics Office, *Homicide Offences,* Cork

Charlesworth, E.A. and Nathan, R.G. (1987) *Stress Management, A Comprehensive Guide to Your Well-being,* London, Corgi

Cameron, Deborah (2009) *The Myth or Mars and Venus,* Oxford University Press, USA

Conaty, Bill and Charan, Ram (2011) *The Talent Masters,* London, Random House Business

Department of Education and Skills (2007) *Se Si Report,* Dublin

Department of Enterprise, Trade and Employment (2002) *The Male/Female Wage Gap in Ireland,* Dublin

Department of Enterprise, Trade and Employment (2007) *Bullying in the Workplace,* Dublin

Equality Authority and the Economic and Social Research Institute (2005) *Gender Inequalities in Time Use: The Distribution of Caring, Housework and Employment Among Women and Men in Ireland,* Department of Justice, Equality and Law Reform, Dublin

Finn, Charles C: *http://www.poetrybycharlescfinn.com*

Gibran, Kahlil (1923) *The Prophet,* Penguin Books, London

Groddeck, Georg (1977) *The Meaning of Illness,* New York, International Universities Press, Inc.

Humphreys, Tony and Ruddle, Helen (2010): *The Compassionate Intentions of Illness,* Cork, Attic Press

Humphreys, Tony and Ruddle, Helen: (2010) *Relationship, Relationship, Relationship, The Heart of A Mature Society,* Cork, Attic Press

Humphreys, Tony (2006) *The Mature Manager – Managing from the Inside Out,* Dublin, Newleaf

Irish Prison Service (2001) *Irish Prison Service Annual Report 2001,* Longford

INTO (2003/2004) http://www.into.ie/ROI/publications/genderimbalance

Kandola, Pearn (2008): *Employers need to ensure their employees understand what constitutes and causes workplace bullying,* Presentation at PSI Annual Conference, Carlow

Males Ireland, http://www.malesireland.com

O'Donohue, John (1999) *Anam Chara*, Bantam, London

O'Donohue, John (2007) *Benedictus*, Bantam, London

Patmore, Angela (2009) *The Truth About Stress,* London, Atlantic Books

Roosevelt, Eleanor (1950) *This is My Story, New York,* Bantam

TUI (2007): http://www.tui.iePublications_and_Reports (September 2007)

United Nations (2010) *Human Development Report,* http://hdr.undp.org/en/reports/global/hdr2010

World Health Organisation:

D*epression,htt*p://www.who.int/mental_health/management/depression/definition/en/

Index